Vincent O'Sullivan

A Quest for Divine Union

By A. M. Panaghis

First Edition

Biographical Publishing Company
Prospect, Connecticut

Vincent O'Sullivan
A Quest for Divine Union

First Edition

Published by:

Biographical Publishing Company
35 Clark Hill Road
Prospect, CT 06712-1011
Phone: 203-758-3661   Fax: 208-247-1493
e-mail: biopub@aol.com

All rights reserved. No part of this book may be reproduced or transmitted in any form or by any means, electronic or mechanical, including photocopying, recording, or by any information storage or retrieval system without the written permission of the author, except for the inclusion of brief quotations in a review.

Copyright © 2001 by A.M. Panaghis
First Printing 2001

PRINTED IN THE UNITED STATES OF AMERICA

Publisher's Cataloging-in-Publication Data

Panaghis, A.M.,
   Vincent O'Sullivan : A Quest for Divine Union / by A.M. Panaghis.-- 1st ed.
   p. cm.
   ISBN 1-929882-18-1
   1. Panaghis, A.M., Analysis of the poetry written by Vincent O'Sullivan. 2. Poetry critique. 3. Religion.   I. Title.
   809

2001092592

DEDICATION

*To the memory of my parents
who gave me love and knowledge*

Table of Contents

Chapter I
    Introduction: The Soul in the Abyss   5

Chapter II
    Poems: The Soul in Heaven's Court   70

Chapter III
    The Houses of Sin: The Soul in God's Embrace   129

Chapter IV
    Conclusion: The Soul in Ecstasy   178

Works Cited   203

Index   208

Chapter 1
Introduction: The Soul in the Abyss

To understand the *fin-de-siècle* one has to look at the work of the writers as well as the social and intellectual events that molded significantly this complex and rich period. A close examination of the literature yields a fuller comprehension of the philosophic concepts and the theological beliefs that prevailed. The aim of this study is to view the poetry of Vincent O'Sullivan as an evolving process by which the poet moves forward and upward simultaneously in an attempt to fulfill the Divine union. To delineate his experience the poet created a religious context within which he expressed his ideas and feelings. Furthermore, O'Sullivan believed that the only way to make his poems effective and interesting was to blend personal with borrowed ideas.[1] As such, the meaning of the poems is conveyed only when they are viewed individually and in the order they appear. Actually, the analysis of the poems in their original order is the only method that yields not only an explanation of the complexities that underline the artist's psyche but also outlines the poet's vision. Finally, the psycho-theological approach used in this study aims at helping the reader not only to come to know O'Sullivan, the man, but also appreciate his work.

The British society of the 1890's had a delusive veneer of peace and material prosperity, but beneath its serene surface dissatisfaction fermented quietly. It was a matter of time before the foundations of the powerful, but complacent, Victorian Empire began to collapse. The writers of the nineties had already detected signs of corrosion and dissolution that had started to shake the social fabric of the Victorian world. As for the glow of the Victorian world it continued to linger a little while longer but as 1914 approached it became fainter and gradually vanished.

Decadence is the term applied to the last two decades of the Victorian period. And like any other decadent period it has all the qualities that mark the end of great periods. There is "an intense self-consciousness, a restless curiosity in research, an over-subtilizing refinement upon refinement, a spiritual and moral perversity." The Decadents were fascinated by any sort of sin that corrupted man's soul and that led to a tragic end. "They sought forgetfulness in vice, and when the sweets of the nameless forbidden fruit were sucked to the dregs the result was total, irremediable *ennui*. The fulfilment of wild desire led to an arid satiety from which, in more than one case, the only escape was death." It is no wonder then that this period is marked by so many "tragedy prone" young men. As a result, most of them died by accident, self-induced disease or their own hand before they reached the age of forty.[2]

The last two decades of the nineteenth century witnessed radical changes not only in society and politics but also in religion and literature. Yet during this period England, which had become a superpower under Queen Victoria's reign began to show signs of disintegration. Men were forced to adjust to new concepts and new systems of government something that was extremely painful for some, and almost impossible for others. The demands of change that kept appearing daily increased the tension and the restlessness that young men, especially, felt. They felt compelled to alter their life style, their religious, political, social ideas, as well as their moral codes. Not only did they feel lost they also felt, at the same time, helpless to resist the flow of change.

Many old ideas about the benefits and honor of imperialism, economic stability, and the unshaken belief in man's supremacy had dissolved as a result of waning confidence in imperial expansion, the bitterness that followed the Boer War, industrial rivalry, and foreign competition. There was a continuous increase of political, economic, and social anxiety. As for the ideas that were not discarded, they were highly and passionately criticized. The general attitude was that of revolution since there was so much talk of change. As such not one political principal, religious dogma, social tradition, or moral code went unquestioned. For the conservative it was an era of all out destruction. The world he believed in and trusted and to which he belonged could not provide him any longer with satisfaction or protection. At the same time, for the conservative it was extremely hard to accept change, and being unable to resist change he felt trapped. He was caught in the middle of conflicting currents that confused and alarmed him. So the new intellectual trends and the social changes found them unprepared since most of their ideas were based on theories that were recorded by writers and thinkers of the early nineteenth century. It is worth mentioning that the beginning of the twentieth century continued to experience the same feeling of uneasiness that prevailed during the *fin-de-siècle*. In this manner the new century carried on the feeling of restlessness which became stronger as 1914 approached and the hope of subduing it was certainly eliminated. The revelation that the common patterns of life and moral values were insufficient never stopped taking people by surprise, but as this recognition intensified the feeling of *ennui* eventually grew.

During the last decades of the nineteenth century England suffered a depression which proved to be a major factor in shaping the nation's future. Hard times hit the prosperous society and everybody thought that the end of the world was very close. Those who took care of the economy tried to explain their hardships as well as find the cause of their problems. As time went by they realized that the root of their economic problems was the rise of younger nations such as the United States that had began to recover from the Civil War, and the united Germany which had began to threaten and challenge England's power. As a result, the British began to criticize the social system, high taxes, high production costs, union demands, higher wages; everything seemed to be responsible for their severe economic problems. On the whole, "the social disorder, economic crisis, and institutional malfunctioning had contributed to the growth of Socialist parties and to the spread of the Marxist doctrine."[3]

The image of England being a modern and progressive nation that had achieved prosperity and offered its people the benefits of higher standards of living was shattered. In the 1880's poverty and new trends in industry, like monopolies and foreign competition, prompted labor leaders to demand higher benefits for the worker. As Socialism began to spread the Labor Party started to gain power. ***The Communist Manifesto*** (1847) and ***Das Capital*** (1867) became the source for writers such as William Morris who believed that a Utopia could be achieved only if the working class strove to take government as well as its own destiny into its hands. At the same time, a wave of labor unrest began to spread as workers demanded wage increases and better working conditions. Finally, strikes and violence became the outward signs of the hidden restlessness which, at that time, they could neither define nor explain. Laissez-faire that had deeply influenced the social and political structure of England was challenged. It was decided that the new economic system had to be controlled if the rights of all social classes were to be safeguarded.

The agricultural depression which plagued England between the years 1870 to 1920 hit the landed gentry and agricultural labor the hardest. It was the changes that occurred in the village that terminated rural England. The idealization of rural life and its values that many writers described and accepted as essential truth and as part of a Utopian world vanished, and now all they could write about was their nostalgia for the lost golden age. However, the lost golden age became a deep yearning for a simpler society that would offer refuge from the harshness of modern civilization. The idea that material gain entailed a perceptible spiritual loss was overwhelming. In fact, this spiritual loss became a significant theme for the writers of the time.

And on the political scene, the nineteenth century was not only an age of imperialism and expansion abroad, but also of democracy within England. Many bills were passed to make life more equal and just for everyone. Outside the borders of England colonialism was practiced and the term "imperialism" was used for the first time on the international scene and meant

> . . . the effort of a state or a person to impose rule. As for the nations of Europe, they took on

the mission of spreading their civilization and culture across the world; therefore, enhancing their prestige, the purely political and legal definition of imperialism was broadened to include psychological and moral considerations.[4]

Max Nordeau in **Degeneration** argued that the "tendencies in literature and art were symptomatic of deterioration and hysteria. This illness had to be exposed so the public would arm itself against such corruptive influences."[5] Holbrock Jackson, on the contrary, claimed that the last decade of the nineteenth century was "a renascent period." A period "characterized by much mental activity and a quickening of the imagination, combined with pride of material prosperity, conquest and imperial expansion as well as the desire for social service and a fuller communal and personal life."[6] Undoubtedly the 1880's was an age of transition. It was "passing not only from one morality to another, but also from one culture to another, and from one religion to a dozen or none. Everyone was running about in a hundred different directions."[7] Jackson also defended the 1890's when he said that it was not totally hopeless or totally decadent. Finally, Jackson rejected Nordeau's disparaging description of the 1890's as degenerate. To Jackson, the nineties was a period of regeneration simply because a lot of what was written at that time was the result of a healthy genius and not an insane one.

The publication of Charles Darwin's **On the Origin of Species** (1859) cast doubt on the prevalent religious belief, particularly man's supremacy in the natural chain of being, by introducing the idea that he was the descendant of the ape. The heated debates that followed Darwin's premises inevitably brought change to the prevailing thought of the time. Darwin's process of evolution pointed out to the survival of the fittest. According to Herbert Spenser the desire to survive was a very normal need especially in economics. That meant that the weak failed and the strong endured and became stronger. Spenser also believed that society eliminated the weak and the unfit, and so naturally the talented and strong remained. Evolution was not necessarily negative since gradually, this tough competitive process would lead ultimately to the development of the ideal man. This same concept of the survival of the few gave rise to the trend of Naturalism. Since survival was for the few, then the rest of the people could do nothing else but drag out their time because fate somehow willed it so. As a consequence of this attitude the idea of death and the mood of despair overwhelmed the 1890's. But there was another consequence to Darwin's theory and that had to do with religious assumptions that the Victorians began to question and doubt. Basic religious concepts such as creation, sin, sacrifice, and redemption were challenged. If there was no creation and man was not put in Paradise, then the whole story of Adam and Eve, the fall, the Original Sin, and Christ's sacrifice and redemption were meaningless. After all, if man had not sinned why was salvation necessary? Why did it matter if man sinned or not? Why did man spend so much of his energy to win the favor of God by doing penance? Why was it essential for man to resist sin and follow a path of virtue in his life so as to attain a life in Heaven? These and so many other questions preoccupied the minds of theologians as well as common people. There was no easy answer to all these questions and when an answer was provided it rarely seemed satisfactory. On the whole, the confusion and restlessness that spread among intellectuals as well as the common people was hard to ignore.

Late nineteenth-century thinkers challenged the basic concepts of previous philosophers by stressing the irrational side of man's personality. According to them impulses, instincts, and desires were more powerful than logic. Frederick Nietzsche advocated the concept of the irrational, and attacked the current belief of his days in reason and restraint because he thought that they were obstacles to fuller experiences. He also criticized Christian morality and refuted the idea that man is essentially good, on the basis that there is no absolute good or evil. Modern bourgeois society was decadent and corrupt, a victim of the excessive development of the rational faculties at the expense of will and instinct. Nietzsche urged man to accept the dark, mysterious world of instincts and desires as the true forces of life. Unfortunately, the great hero who would become a "superman" was still to be born. Whenever that happened, the new hero/leader would lay down his laws and values and courageously break away from the traditional values and morality. Generally speaking, there was a deep need or desire to become virtuous individuals by pursuing inner virtue. The Decadent writers who were influenced by the instability and fluidity of the times challenged the conception of human rationality as faulty. Reason set strict limits on man's will, impulses, and instincts in other words, man's unconscious was to be avoided since dark forces dwelled there. These powerful forces of the unconscious were proven more potent than reason and logic. By turning to emotion, impulses, instincts, and desires the writers of the nineties, like the Romantics before them, indirectly stated that their literature would be different from that of the Victorians. The fact that they stressed these forces and considered the unconscious an exhaustive source of materials to draw from set them apart from their contemporaries right away. Furthermore, what is interesting is that this new direction in literature reflected a shift in behavior and lifestyle as well. No wonder then the writers of the nineties were referred to as daring, immoral, and dangerous and had to be ostracized for the protection of the public.

Henri Bergson was one of many thinkers who attacked positivism. He mocked the claim that science could explain and satisfy human needs. According to him "the method of intuition, whereby the mind strives for an immanent relationship with the object, to become one with it, and tell us more about reality" was more effective and productive than the method of analysis employed by science. He also believed that intuition is far more efficient a method for knowledge acquisition than scientific methods. Lastly, he stated that the mind is not a collection of atoms operating according to mechanical principles, but an active consciousness with profound intuitive capacities.[8] Naturally Bergson's ideas, which were considered revolutionary appealed immensely to the writers of the nineties and without ado they applied them in their work.

Besides Bergson psychologists, too, were preoccupied with the significance of intuition. Sigmund Freud, for instance, focused on the power of the non-rational drives in man. Unlike Nietzsche, he recognized the potential danger of these irrational forces. He believed that these forces had to be regulated for the benefit of society. He respected the value of reason and believed that man's behavior was governed by these inner hidden forces rather than reason. Freud developed the theory of the *id*, the seat of the unconscious, where man's instincts constantly strive to assert themselves. What happens when the *id* is denied an outlet? Well, when this energy is frustrated anger and dissatisfaction result. But to gratify the *id* entails ultimate pleasure that is detrimental to civilized society. Freud also maintained that evil was rooted in human nature it did not exist outside of man or society. Some thinkers were of the opinion that education had the power to equip man with knowledge but fell short of eliminating evil from his nature. As for Freud he argued that man should become aware of his true nature, particularly of the evil aspect in him, even though that might lead him to despair. Finally, man has to learn to repress the unconscious because, Freud believed, if it was let loose it would disrupt the workings of the *ego* and the *superego* that are responsible for channeling the energy of the *id* in an orderly and acceptable manner.

One of the major instincts Freud examined extensively is that of death. He viewed it as a return to the original organic state of total and complete freedom from any kind of tension. Tension as he explained is the result of the everlasting conflict between the *id* and the *ego*, as well as between the *ego* and the *superego*. Under these circumstances death becomes the desired state because it offers a way out of the tension; in other words, death is a release. Often the death instinct is released through drugs, drinking, and ultimately committing suicide. Deep in man's heart there is the desire to attain the pre-existing state where tension does not exist and harmony prevails. Death seems to be the means to achieve this harmonious state. "The existence of the death instinct culminates in the emergence of aggression, in the wish of the individual to either destroy others or himself."[9] Freud's influence is clear in the writings of many *fin-de-siecle* writers. It is evident that the concept of death as a release from tension and conflict appealed to many of the writers of the nineties. Not only did they use it in their work, they also believed that it could offer the desired escape from the restlessness and torment of their lives. Without a doubt death was an attractive state that could provide an end and a beginning. For the religiously oriented writer it was the way to eternal happiness in heaven, and for the irreligious, it was an end to earthly suffering.

After Freud, Carl Jung developed his multi-faceted theory of the collective unconscious. He held the view that the collective unconscious was the source of myths and symbols shared by all. The *id*, which for Freud was the seat of all aggression, for Jung was more than just the seat of libidinous forces, it was where the history of the human race existed. He thought that the unconscious has to be fully experienced if man is to achieve self-knowledge. The collective unconscious is not an "undifferentiated mass of material," but organized in its "manifestations by recurring patterns called archetypes."[10] The concept of the *self*, the duality of the *animus* and the *anima*, the process of individuation that he postulated were used by the writers of the 1890's and later on by twentieth-century artists. Furthermore, he distinguished between the extroverted and introverted man on the basis of the four functions of the mind: thinking, feeling, sensation, and intuition. One or more of these four functions prevailed in each individual and shaped his personality.

The theories of both Freud and Jung presented a

different kind of reality from that prevalent heretofore. This new level of reality was associated with the psychic self that rejects the outer, physical reality that dominates it. The Impressionists, Decadents, Aesthetes, and Symbolists were all attracted by this unknown and obscure world that existed in the deep layers of the human psyche and not somewhere out there. This new reality is what these writers tried to portray as concretely as possible in their work.

The years 1880-1900 reflect a turning point in English literature. The deep need for a spiritual renewal that had become an issue for consideration on a national consciousness was present in the works of these writers. In order to achieve this spiritual rebirth intuition was emphasized, mysticism revived, and philosophy and psychology examined for new ways and answers. Many concepts and attitudes underwent change as the artist retired from the busy world to his lonely ivory tower, but not to nature as the Romantics had done before him. One look at the literature of the nineties shows that the lonely artists withdrew from the bustle of the day but never left the city actually, they were known to come forth at night to wander in the streets of the city. As their poetry proves most of the writers wrote about the city and the multiple social problems of the time. Amongst others, Richard Le Gallienne wrote *A Ballad of London* and *Sunset in the City*, John Davidson, too, devoted his poem *London* to the city, and both Lord Alfred Douglas and Arthur Symons wrote about the city at night in *Impression du Nuit*, and *City Nights* respectively. The rise of the new Romanticism in the 1880's was freed from intellectual restraint that stifled its growth. Its inner impulse carried it either to the most dissimilar beliefs, or to a kind of hedonism, which found a bittersweet pleasure in absolute negation. In this wide vista one detects a variety of tendencies at work. For example, there is the sensuous poetry of Algernon Swinburne on the one hand, and the mystical verses of Francis Thompson on the other. And in prose there is the excitement of adventure in the novels of Robert Louis Stevenson, but also bitter naturalism in the work of George Gissing. Finally, one should not ignore the aesthetic experiences of Oscar Wilde and the rich ornamental style of Walter Pater.

The Yellow Book became the epitome of everything that was shocking, puzzling, and delightful to the people of the time. It became the symbol of the bizarre, the queer in art and life as well as of everything that was considered modern. And as the Decadents searched for ultimate truth they were reminded of Thomas Carlyle's definition of the imaginative man who is "priest and prophet to lead us heavenward or magician and wizard to lead us hellward."[11] Like the Romantics Carlyle believed that if the imagination were allowed to operate in its own right it would "transform our lives." To him "the state of illumination, or truly understanding, fundamental to man and the world, is to ordinary life as waking is to sleeping, or open to closed eyes."[12] The concept of the imagination had a deep impact on the writers of the nineties, including Vincent O'Sullivan, who believed that it was the faculty that helped man perceive the world around him, truth, and the overwhelming beauty of heaven.

Toward the end of the nineteenth century artists felt that literature and art were moving into a new phase, and that, even though Queen Victoria was still on the throne of England, the complacent Victorian era was coming to an end. There was a strong belief that all established intellectual, moral, and social forms were vanishing, and that the new situations required new attitudes. In art two powerful trends clashed. The first, held by John Ruskin and G. B. Shaw who believed that art should be created for the common man, to offer solutions to his problems as well as to entertain him. The second, espoused by James M. Whistler and Oscar Wilde, claimed that the mission of art was to elevate man by refusing to come down to common taste or ideas.

In the Victorian age the artist was considered a member of society while the Decadent artist was treated as an outcast. As such the Decadent artist had to deal with a hostile world, a world similar to that which the Romantics confronted before him. Looking back at *the fin-de-siècle*, no one can dispute the fact that the seeds of twentieth-century literature were sown by these artists who had experienced the complexities, the bitterness, the fears, and the doubts of the times. Yet critics such as Max Nordeau insisted on labeling these artists as immoral. He fervently believed that society had to be warned of them because their work had the potential to destroy civilized society. Moreover, he objected to the doctrine of art for art's sake because it was responsible for "artistic voluptuousness."[13] Finally, Nordeau stressed the fact that an artist who devoted himself to aesthetics was unable to contribute anything of value to society.

The England reflected in the literature of the nineties is not a strong giant instead it is a superpower in the process of self-discovery. This means that many artists realized that change in human affairs was a necessity and of vital importance. Of course this does not mean that change could not be unpredictable, excessive, uncontrollable, or even destructive. As has already been mentioned this was a period of social, cultural, and ideological change and the artists not only depicted these changes but also explored new possibilities and ideas in their work.

Monroe C. Beardsley, in his book **Aesthetics: Problems in the Philosophy of Criticism** says:

> . . . it is the view that aesthetic objects are not subject to moral judgment, that only aesthetic categories can be, or ought to be, applied to them. Not because they are objects rather than acts, for it may be granted that objects can become subject to moral judgment when the presence affects behavior, but because according to the view we are now considering the side-effects of aesthetic objects, if any, need not be taken into account.[14]

The aesthetic movement promoted a philosophy of artistic freedom from conventional restraints as well as innovation to content and form with a deep belief in art for art's sake. Emphasis was laid on sensory perception, the appreciation of beauty, the presentation of mood, and the perfection of technical expression, rather than morality. The extensive and free use of aesthetics led to loss of control and consequently, in some cases, to perversity of literary form and content. And even though aestheticism was often misused for different reasons the fact that it appeared as a rebellion against the status quo of the Victorian period cannot be overlooked.

The aesthetic movement of the 1880's began in Britain as a revolt against the ugliness of the industrial age and the strict moral Victorian standards. "The art produced was totally independent of any moral, philosophical, or cultural concerns to the extent that it finally turned into an art of perversity." The artist of the nineties rebelled against the poetic role of the Victorian artist. His aim was not to educate or amuse but to shock, to present a "rescued fragment" of life and to "reveal the substance of truth."[15] Artists firmly believed that the revelation of truth required new techniques but also a very sophisticated reader who would be able to interpret and criticize correctly. One can say that the aesthetic movement stood for individualism as opposed to conformity, sensibility, or morality. Art for art's sake had no didactic purpose in mind, after all these artists scoffed at everything traditional or moral. The aesthetes demanded from readers to reject the traditional texts and accept the new ones with an open mind. This meant the readers they sought had to be willing to develop a taste for the new literature.

The Decadents lived at the end of the nineteenth century, a period of peculiar crisis and disintegration. These artists reflected in their work a sense of doom and extinction that haunted the whole generation. They manifested in both their lives and work a highly stylized manner, a fascination with morbidity and perversity, an attitude of *ennui*, and a preference for an artificial style rather than a natural or conventional one. On the contrary, the aesthetes created fantastical and artificial worlds by which they escaped from their surroundings and materialism that tainted everything. They declared their individuality by expressing their own visions of beauty. In the process they explored feelings of despair, degeneration, alienation, morbid and perverse sexuality, as well as mystical and religious themes. On the whole, they were not interested in the general but rather in the particular which eventually helped them create dream worlds in which they lost themselves. The spirit of Decadence together with the style of Aestheticism is detected in almost all of the literature of the nineties. Unquestionably, Decadent doom and Aesthetic artificiality blended to produce the unique literature of the 1890s.

The artist of the *fin-de-siècle* having been alienated from society reacted by taking on the pose of a "dandy" or a "bohemian." As he looked back and saw an obscure past he was forced to turn for elegance to the present where, to his disappointment, discovered there was none to be found. But when it was time to look ahead he was seized by fear because he realized that there was no future for him, somehow he was doomed to extinction. In his work he refused to accept existing conventions and experimented continuously in an effort to find the perfect and most suitable technique that would fully express his feelings and thoughts. As a bohemian he was compelled to flee from society into exotic fantasy islands. Since he felt uncomfortable with the culture of his time he had to create an abstract, imaginary life different from the reality of the mundane world. Lothar Honinghausen says:

> The interest of the late nineteenth-century artists in occultism has to be seen in the historical context. Estranged equally from the materialistic age and religious orthodoxy, but driven by vague spiritual desires they display a half-serious, half-playful interest in occult practices and mystic systems fascinated by mystery and transcendent reality.[16]

The occult, thought the artist of the nineties, was worth exploring and the hope that it might yield a reality and a world wherein he would find peace of mind and freedom of expression intensified. So the artist drifted in the mysterious world of the occult expecting that he might be able to alleviate his despair. Unfortunately, all he succeeded in doing was increase his already existing confusion even more. On the other hand, the aesthetes recognized no duties, pursued no interests, and were indifferent to religion, morality, politics, and even society. They seemed abnormal, selfish, and irresponsible to a society that stressed work and social service. They vaunted themselves as different from middle class society and pursued beauty as they sought to satisfy themselves within their ivory towers.[17]

Decadence is a term that has been widely discussed. In most cases, it deals with the decline of previously held personal and social values. The Decadents did not care about the future because they believed that there was none. Instead they stressed the present which they regarded as disappointing and that, drove them to develop a sense of cynicism and nihilism that they upheld and expressed in their work. A number of artists tried to describe the conflict they underwent as they placed themselves alongside the common man. They created poetry that revealed the new situations and the new truths they envisioned. Another group of poets who withdrew to the realm of ideal beauty and portrayed only the perspective of it in their work disregarded the confusion of the majority. And yet, others often tried to fuse their own sense of beauty with reality but that proved to be not only painful but also impossible. Finally, it should be pointed out that a number of Decadent artists were prone to extremes, especially in the pursuit of pleasure. Many of them turned instinctively to images of the grotesque to convey a sense of falling, of lost direction, and even of madness.

It is indisputable that the *fin-de-siecle* foreshadows the fragmentation and alienation of the twentieth century. The heroes of decadent art were physically and mentally crippled, passive, vulnerable, abused victims who did not try to maintain any sense of dignity. They lived for the sadistic enjoyment of their own misery and did not strive for any amelioration of their situation. Detached from the community and attracted only to a frightening madness and a bizarre world of beauty, they led a confused, unfulfilled, and incomplete life.

The 1890's became known as the age of decay and dissolution. No wonder then it was described as pale, yellow in color, sick, and ailing. There was not the slightest sign that this period would ever beget the glow that made the Victorian era so impressive any time soon. It is noteworthy that this age succeeded in discovering the cause of its ailment. Its diagnosed illness was no other but the Victorian life style, Victorian morality, and Victorian ideology. Nonetheless, the *fin-de-siecle* is also considered a transitional period because it exists between the great and stable Victorian period and the shattered and fragmented Modern age. It is the period in which the great, robust, and healthy Victorian Empire began to dwindle and soon was to be extinct.

The poets of the 1890's decided to examine the cause of their despondency as well. They thought it was time they stopped wallowing in the complacency of the Victorians. It dawned on them that they had to act because that was the only way they could free themselves from the ambuscade of sickness and dissolution. Gradually, they were shocked to find out that there was nothing they could do to rid themselves of the moral and spiritual sterility that had become their doom. It was as if they were suffering from an incurable disease that drove most of them to their early death. Doubt, endless questioning, and frustration led them to drugs, alcohol, and suicide. The Decadents of the 1890's, according to Holbrock Jackson, were not so degenerate as "to have lost hope in future joy or to have had full faith in their attainment of it." For Jackson it is natural for a generation under pressure because of scientific discoveries and material prosperity to embody "a tired mood, and reject hope," Furthermore, it is common to take "a subtle joy in playing with fire and calling it sin; in scourging themselves for an unholy delight, in tasting the bitter-sweet of actions potent with remorse."[19]

The nineties came to be characterized by a plethora of ideas to choose from, accept, reject, or interpret in whatever way. It was at this time that the principle of relativity in connection to ideas already there created confusion and consequent despair. Yet in some cases, the Decadents were intoxicated by these new ideas and tried to tackle many of them in their work. The poets of the *fin-de-siècle* were desperately seeking for solutions to their problems. They thought of the Victorians as a poor, blind, complacent people, who were torn by doubt, were spiritually bewildered, and were lost in a troubled universe. But there was a small group of poets, including O'Sullivan, who were excessively religious, lamentably idealistic, deeply nostalgic of the past, and ready to forego present delights for the vision of a world beyond.

"No one has ever passed twice over the same stream. Nay, the passenger himself is without identity. Upon the same stream at the same moment we do, and do not embark, for we are, and are not."[20] Walter Pater used this statement to explain the Heraclitean principle of constant change known as the Doctrine of Motion. In this context all things give way to change and nothing remains the same. Pater argues that the philosophy of the nonconsecutive, the incoherent, the insane, contains the seeds of scientific ideas, of the most modern metaphysical as well as the most modern empirical philosophies.

In the doctrine of the "Perpetual Flux" Pater stresses the principle of evolution, of constant change, and of disintegration. Pater describes the principle of evolution as a process of recognition that brings wisdom which reaches from end to end, sweetly and strongly ordering all things.[21] All that is, is not really, because it is always becoming. Thus nothing is absolute and everything is relative. By stressing the doctrine of motion Pater showed that things are in a state of continuous flux, and evolution. A constant motion, change and disintegration, an ever-ceasing becoming toward a universal integration made experience essential for man in his attempt to achieve a state of being. Hence Pater emphasizes the importance of burning always "with this hard, gem-like flame," to continue to burn with this flame is interpreted as "success in life."[22]

O'Sullivan borrowed Pater's views of motion to convey the progress of the soul from Hell to Heaven. Becoming and change were essential if man's soul was to achieve a state of eternal being in God's embrace. Without motion the human soul would neither leave Hell nor Purgatory and Heaven would remain unreachable. Without change the human soul would not shed sin, repent, get purified, and finally, unite with the Divine. According to O'Sullivan the soul had to disintegrate, a state attained by separating from the flesh, before the final integration and assimilation with the Divine occurred. The idea of disintegration the poet borrowed from Jung. In psychology disintegration is necessary if the process of individuation is to take place. By fusing Pater's philosophy with Jung's psychology O'Sullivan acquired a special method by which to explain his own religious vision. It is this psycho-theological method that makes his poetry different from that of other *fin-de-siècle* writers.

Pater continued to expound his influential theory further when he said that it is experience that matters in all its details and factuality, unique and individual as it is, never a means and always an end in itself because it is ever changing. And Pater goes on to add that what matters, is "not the fruit of experience, but experience itself."[23] Thus experience becomes an end in itself. It is no wander then that all writers in the nineties who espoused Pater's philosophy and chose to apply it were expected to have acquired the appropriate experience as well, otherwise their writings would lack intrigue a quality that appealed to the reader of the time. Many writers used their imagination to come up with the most shocking, or macabre, or unusual experiences. Interestingly, these were experiences that no human being could go through because they were simply too extreme. Yet the writers who wrote about such extreme experiences and identified with their daring heroes, ended up either driving readers away because their work was considered immoral, or attracting them because their work was different, bold, and novel. Even though some of these writings were banned from bookshelves many went to great lengths to find a copy simply because such works offered, the desperate and restless Victorian, an escape through the wanderings of vivid imagination. Kindling the readers' imagination was the aim of some of these innovative writers who believed that once the imagination awakened then man could reach outside the boundaries of his apathetic society and maybe, just maybe, discover a way to save himself.

Pater also applied the concept of relativity to reality. Reality is in fact an individual man's experience of a single moment or a single impression. What is real now will not be real later, for in every life "every hour is unique, changed altogether by a stray word, or glance, or touch" and "every moment some mood or passion or insight or intellectual excitement is irresistibly real and attractive to us for that moment only."[24] The absolute is irrelevant to experience and to rapid change. This state of perpetual flux makes all knowledge wholly relative and in a way impossible, and "turns ascertained truth into a dead letter."[25] Unless knowledge becomes part of our experience it is not knowledge at all. For we know only what we experience, personally, individually, and that only for the time we experience it. So knowledge, like reality, is relative, differing from one man to another, and from one moment to another in the life of the same man. In the work of every writer there is an interpretation of reality, his own personal interpretation. The fact that most of the writers of the nineties wanted to experience their own reality was as important as creating their own conventions to express it. The Decadents were inventive, adventurous, and even inquisitive; that led often to the discovery of a new reality. In this "large tolerance the spirit of the renaissance worked through mind and imagination inspiring artists with a new confidence in themselves and courage to take risks."[26]

Experience itself does not consist only of objects invested by language, impressions, unstable, flickering, inconsistent, and in perpetual flight. Experience means much more since every one of these impressions is the impression of the individual in his isolation, so that the whole scope of reality, of knowledge, is dwarfed into the narrow chamber of the individual mind. That is how man, the individual, becomes "the measure of all things," each mind keeping as a solitary prisoner its own dream of the world. The duty of the artist is not to depict the world as it is, but to give expression to that personal relative world. What is really meaningful is the artist's impression of fact, of the world, in the final analysis his vision where all really begins and ends.[27]

"Just in proportion as the writer's aim" Pater declares in his essay *On Style* "consciously or unconsciously, comes to be the transcribing, not of the world, not of mere fact, but of his sense of it, he becomes an artist, and his work fine art."[28] The material of art is not absolute, but relative fact, "fact in its infinite variety, as modified by human preference in all its infinitely varied forms, and each fact is a representation connected with the soul, of a specific personality, in its preferences, its volition and power."[29]

"Beauty, like all other qualities presented to human experience, is relative," Pater writes in the Preface to the **Renaissance**, "and the definition of it becomes meaningless and useless in proportion to its abstractness."[30] Beauty unquestionably is unique and independent. To ask what beauty is or what is its relation to truth "are metaphysical questions as unprofitable as metaphysical questions elsewhere."[31] Beauty, in the context of O'Sullivan's poetry, is spiritual and associated only with God and the soul after it recovers the light of purity. Rarely does the poet use earthly beauty and when he does, it is for the sole purpose of juxtaposing heavenly beauty or conveying the theme of temptation. The persona is expected to withstand earthly beauty and turn his attention to heavenly beauty.

"Art provides man with a special, unique, impression of pleasure."[32] Unique because it is of a specific use to us in a life that consists of a group of impressions, unstable, flickering, inconsistent, which burn and are extinguished without our being conscious of them. Art, says Pater, is moral because it is beautiful, because it can create order out of disorder by blending material from life to its purpose, by transmitting matter into form. In this lies the special, unique impression of pleasure which is the very essence of the aesthetic experience and which gives it its unique value.

Herbert Gerber states that "at the end of centuries . . . human beings, but artists in particular, are infected by a sense of death, decay, agony, old gods falling, cultural decline on the one hand, or by a sense of regeneration on the other."[33] However disoriented, fragmented and troubled this era was, still it was marked by extraordinary creativity in thought and the arts.[34] In art there was a departure from the strict Victorian literary themes. Writers such as George Gissing, A. E. Housman, and Thomas Hardy dealt with new themes. Gissing was concerned with the increasingly depressing conditions of urban existence and the alienation of the artist. Housman, who believed to be doomed by love and fate, confronted the sense of fatality he shared with Gissing and even with Joseph Conrad and others, with stoicism. Hardy, often as pessimistic in spirit as Gissing, and as devoted to the English rural life as Housman, introduced these themes in his novels. As for G. B. Shaw he revolted against the sentimental play and its conventions. He dealt, instead, with modern issues and tried to offer solutions that proved confusing at times.

The Victorians believed in the artist's ability to provide a moral base for the public. The artist was thought to be a man with a mission, and a member of society who was expected to offer solutions to complex problems. The Romantics before them viewed the artist as an individual who had to run away to nature or withdraw to his ivory tower in an attempt to obtain a vision that would help him and others. When the Romantic retired to the countryside he hoped to create works that would capture the ideal world, and, at the same time, immortalize his vision. Obviously the use of the subjective mode ruled out any intention of conveying a message to his readers. The Decadents differed from the Romantics because, even though they withdrew to their own perverse tower and chose solitude in their wanderings, they continued to walk the dark streets of the city during the night. The Decadents, unlike the Victorians, not only could they not offer solutions to problems but they were also of the opinion that that was not expected of the artist. Moreover, they had chosen to follow the new trend of art for art's sake that ruled out didacticism. After all, how could they offer solutions when they had only doubts and questions. The artist's duty was to create beauty, evoke pleasure, or even shock and in this manner present the reader with an escape from the ugliness and boredom of the physical world. Followers of Oscar Wilde believed that to convey a moral was awfully immoral. E. A. Poe's words that man yearns throughout his life for "supernal beauty" and the artist could satisfy or quench this desire by creating a work of beauty rang loudly in the ears of the Decadent artists[35] Finally, the Decadent artist believed fervently in experiencing beauty fully. All he had to do was transform his sense impressions into a work of art that would excite the soul of any man and evoke pleasure.

    John Ruskin stressed beauty and appealed to the artists of the time when he expressed the view that "in art lay the only means by which modern society could be redeemed and the world made a decent place for man to work and live."[36] The Decadents rejected that view. On the contrary, Dante Gabriel Rosetti, who pursued beauty for its own sake, was appreciated immensely by them. Rosetti's art was divorced of any social meaning; instead it was full of introspection and infinite pain. The sorrow the Decadents experienced for failing to achieve the infinite was heart-breaking, but that did not stop them; on the contrary, it prompted them to continue to search for that happy state they dreamed of and which for some was fantastical, for others spiritual, and for yet others, sensual.

The writers of the nineties lived for long in the dark world of their unconscious as a result it was very difficult for them to return to the world of the conscious and normality. This withdrawal was considered to be a sign of rebellion against Victorian hypocrisy. What they were not aware of was that their rebellion made them debutantes in a very dangerous game that they could not control. As time went by they slipped deeper and deeper into despair and darkness and illusion became their reality. A reality that was relative and changeable since everything is in a state of flux. In addition, it was a reality that continuously changed under the intoxication of drugs. It was a reality that became morose and morbid as the Decadents got into the habit of acting out their obsessions and perversions. The reality they created had the potential to lead them to insanity, but they preferred it to Victorian reality, which they found hard to handle. Hence a logical inference would suggest that escaping and living forever in an unreal world was highly dangerous yet, a return to the present world proved excruciating and intolerable.

The artists of the time never thought of giving up their perverse lifestyle or changing their attitude. As they withdrew from society and looked within they concentrated on both their self and soul. Inevitably they were bound to stress the spiritual, metaphysical, and psychological aspects at the expense of the social. Their work, therefore, is full of their obsessions, their fears, and their feelings. It is personal and subjective and very different from the literature of the Victorians. As a matter of fact, it is this personal feature that makes the literature of the *fin-de-siècle* unique and attractive to critics. If one is to understand the element of insanity or perversion on which some of that literature is based one ought to ask whether these elements are real, an attitude, a pose, or all of these together? Or does any of the elements depend on the emotions of the writer at any given time? What is definitely real is the fact that these artists tried to lift the veil of appearances only to find themselves caught up in the world they had created and used to impress others. The world they created sprung from the obsessions and fears that crowded their unconscious. To them this world was so real especially when it was transformed into a web which spread its net and trapped them. Ironically, they felt happy and safe in it. Whenever they tried to disentangle themselves from the vicious snare, they found themselves in a world that was too harsh for them, a world which they failed to understand for it was so foreign to them and they had become so alien to it. Consequently, they preferred to stay ambushed in their own world simply because they found peace and security there. The assumption that the element of perversion or insanity was a pose that they used to shock and shake their audience out of their lethargy is a certainty. Each author tried to be more of a sensationalist than the rest in the manner in which he expressed ideas, for example, what the church considered sinful was encouraged and exalted by the Decadents.

Shocking descriptions of sexual perversions and the impressive allurements of powerful death became the order of the day. Neither shocking descriptions nor sexual perversions had ever been touched upon before by any Victorian writer. As a result it was not unnatural to consider writers who wrote about these subjects dangerous to social morality. It was this social denial that encouraged the decadents to use exaggeration in their work, a practice from which they derived pleasure. At the same time, one can say that the more they were criticized for their attitude and ideas the more daring they became in their expressions. Of course, this same denial drove them to slip deeper and deeper into despondency. The fact that they felt outcasts in a society they loathed did not really bother them but surely it was one more reason that prompted them to satirize more severely the Victorian era.

The Decadents tried to turn their life into works of art. They lived a full and sensual life and described their sensual experiences colorfully and in a decorative style. They were aware that their experiences sprung from their unconscious and, therefore, they needed new means of expression. Some found new modes of expression in symbolism. Using symbols helped them objectify their personal experience and give it multiple meanings. Describing events where the hero or persona tasted recurrently the forbidden fruit, emptied his cup to the lees, and wallowed deeply in sin became the best way to awaken the audience from their complacency. They firmly believed that if everyone tried to turn his life into art, then the world would awaken to a new sensibility of beauty and would be a wonderful place to live in. The Decadents found themselves at an impasse even though they were situated in the mainstream of ideological change. Their only recourse was to turn within and look for a special kind of reality to cling to. Whatever they had to say was always presented in the form of a mask or a reflection in the mirror. As such the writers would take on various masks depending on the experience they wanted to convey. The various masks were ephemeral and changeable and were used by the artist to arouse the interest of the reader in his work and life.

    The Victorians before them did not use any masks or mirror reflections to convey their ideas. Alfred Tennyson's *Lady of Shalott* is an example of that. The Lady of Shalott causes the mirror "to crack from side to side" because she could not continue looking at the reflection of reality.[57] As a matter of fact, she was dissatisfied with the reflection of reality. Her yearning to face reality cost her life. On the contrary, the Decadents had no reality to cling to since they believed that physical reality did not exist. And for those who believed that there was some kind of reality out there they also believed that it was influenced by the principle of flux so it was ever changing and never the same. As the century was coming to a close, they wondered if they would live to see another sunrise. Therefore, one can safely argue that for the Decadents there were two types of reality: emotional reality and imaginative reality. The first is hard to define and see since it is internal; and the second is easy to perceive and define, but only by the faculty of the imagination. It is that second type of reality that may be transformed into a work of art. Outside art it seems unlikely that these two realities would fuse. Rabindranath Tagore in his book ***The Religion of Man*** says that "truth is the infinite pursued by science" and reality is "the definition of the infinite which relates truth to the person." He views art as "the response of man's creative soul to the call of the Real."[37]

As has already been pointed out earlier, Arthur Symons argued that the Decadent era had all the qualities that mark the end of great periods.[38] Therefore, it is not surprising that often the Decadents searched for new excitement or oblivion in alcohol, sex, and drugs. The result was that some poets chose a lifestyle of oblivion, others chose to expose a life of doom and as such concur with the statement that they were poets of the tragic generation, and yet others, preferred to be *Poètes Maudits*. Symons notes that man usually finds his "escape from this sterile annihilating reality, in many dreams, in religion, passion, art, each a symbol of forgetfulness, each a symbol of creation, religion being a creation of a new heaven and earth, the creation of heaven out of earth."[39] In this light religion appears as a way out not on the ground of pure belief and piety but on the ground of utility. This view is similar to O'Sullivan's who used religion together with art and dreams as an escape and not as the result of fervent belief. Symons also argued convincingly that a few artists chose religion as a form of escape from the innumerable calamities they faced.[40] Aubrey Beardsley, too, tried to define the artist's dilemma when he said that the artist is "a man caught between two opposite and apparently incompatible pulls." On the one hand, the artist "is drawn by the world and its necessities, while on the other, he yearns toward the Eternal, the Ideal community."[41] Since art is considered an escape from the sickness of the age then under no circumstances could it imitate life. For this group of artists the world was not worth noticing; so, they were motivated to create private worlds in which they found shelter from the ever-changing world around them and the excruciating reality of the *fin-de siècle*. Furthermore, Symons believed that "art may be served by morality; it can never be its servant. For the principles of art are eternal, while the principles of morality mutate with the spiritual ebb and flow of the ages."[42] Symons expressed his opinion about art when he wrote that "the classic is indeed the supreme art--those qualities of perfect simplicity, perfect sanity, perfect proportion, the supreme qualities--then this representative literature today, interesting, beautiful, novel as it is, is really a new and beautiful and interesting disease."[42]

Even though the Decadents, are not a clearly outlined group, the spirit of the *fin-de-siècle* is diffused in all of them. Pessimism, intellectual anarchy, all the pain which usually is found clinging to naturalism, and all the boldness and perversity of aestheticism converge to define the Decadents, but also to show their confusion. They argued that after so many positive achievements man no longer deemed it possible to add a new zest to his efforts. By giving up all thought of further progress the Decadents accepted the law of gradual dissolution. At that time, Charles Beaudelaire, Arthur Rimbaud and Paul Verlaine furnished a peculiar frame of mind and along with it the models and conventions for its expression. Symons described the source of his materials as follows

> The moods of men! There I find my subject, the region over which art rules, and whatever has been a mood of mine, though it has been no more than a ripple on the sea, and had no longer than that ripple's duration, I claim the right to render, if I can, in verse, and I claim, from my critics and readers, the primary understanding, that a mood is after all but a mood, a ripple on the sea, and perhaps with no longer than that ripple's duration.[43]

Even though the Decadents differ drastically from one another still there are certain features that unite them. For example, in all there is a depiction of a psychological outbreak of powerful instincts that had been repressed by the constraints of the Victorian period. There is a social and moral discipline that had been stirred by ferments that had remained calm on the surface. There is also the outcome of a fundamental revolt against the Victorian orthodoxy of conduct, thought, and taste that shook faith. Furthermore, there is a rebellion against accepted morals, a limitless assertion of individuality, a need for convincing truths, an admiration for the French poets, and an acceptance of the whims of the imagination as well as the power of the senses and feelings. One or all of these characteristics are found in the work of the Decadents, and it is this tendency to include one or all of these features that unites them under the label of Decadent poets. Thus the 1890's is a period of English literary history that has been extensively discussed. Fondly or with horror the survivors have recalled the troublesome decade while modern critics have scrutinized its ambiguities with emotions quite diverse. Each artist influenced with his experience or by some particular theory of literary criticism the literature of the period.[44]

    The Decadents borrowed from Realism the technique of depicting reality as minutely and as faithfully as possible no matter how harsh it was. So those who dealt with social themes depicted the problems the English society had to grapple with and, most specifically, stressed the state of the poor in the hope that their audience would be awakened into doing something to relieve the pain and misery that infiltrated the underclass. From Naturalism they adopted the principle of fate, and for those writers who identified with the downtrodden, they too, believed that they were destined to go on living in despair and misery. They stressed the fact that somehow they, too, were victims of society and their own heredity. But Naturalism did not provide all the necessary means of expression the Decadents needed so they looked to Symbolism and began to study the use of symbols. Poets such as Charles Beaudelaire, Arthur Rimbaud, Edgar Allan Poe, and William Blake were closely scrutinized because they used symbols successfully to present the unconscious. Moreover, they were convinced that because symbols were multi-leveled and open to many interpretations their use would enrich their work and add to it an element of mysteriousness thus, making it attractive to the demanding reader of the time. Finally, from Impressionism the Decadents took the method of stringing together inconsequential impressions. The method of capturing impressions from experience and storing them in memory where they would be colored by mood and feeling appealed to them. So they went ahead to select from the stream of time impressions that were sensual, mysterious, and sometimes, morbid.

By the end of the nineteenth century the artist was not concerned with the object itself anymore. As the object receded to the background the interest shifted to the artist's feelings and impressions of the object. The artist's imagination molded and colored the objects that ceased to exist in the external world. After all, the artist was only preoccupied with the complexities of his inner world, so how he responded to the object was what really mattered. It was time for the artist to retreat into his inner world because it was the source of his material, it was the touchstone of understanding reality, and finally, it was the object he was trying to describe and convey.

During the nineties the belief in art for art's sake was strong. Art was to be accepted without any questions. There was no necessity for asking about its advantage or disadvantage to man or society. To the aesthetes art was better than life and the artist was required to capture the beautiful, not the gruesome, aspect of reality. As a result the idea that man is petty but when he creates beauty he becomes a semi-god spread widely. It is no wonder then that the artist as a man deified in his art was a concept that appealed to most Decadents.

It has been said that the Decadents were hedonists with a bad conscience. Many of them were sinners who, even though they threw themselves into the arms of the Catholic Church hoping to be saved, failed to shed the feeling that they were doomed forever. Love for them was the essence of the forbidden, the fall of man, and the irreparable loss of innocence. Their attitude explains why they sympathized with the prostitute. The fact that the bourgeois family rejected her made her attractive to the Decadents. She was considered an outlaw because her lifestyle was a revolt against the institutions of family and church. She represented a storm of passion amidst a society that was cold, and yet all along she was and remained the superior spectator of the lust that she awakened. In the meantime, she felt lonely and apathetic when others were enraptured and intoxicated by her. She became, in brief, a viable female double for some artists.[45] O'Sullivan, too, not only deals with the theme of prostitution in *Papillions du Pavé* as a social phenomenon, but he also chooses to identify with her fate and loneliness.

Some of the Decadents used medieval models and forms besides aestheticism. They remained committed to the idealism inspired by Dante's Beatrice and the unattainable dream world that is expressed by the Platonic ideas. They envisioned an Arcadia where man would transcend and go beyond the futility of life. Religious themes and ideas were used by a number of Decadent poets, including O'Sullivan, in an attempt to express personal spiritual experiences. However, by replacing reality with art all of these artists proved that they were influenced immensely by the social, psychological, and spiritual awareness of their age in their effort to adjust to the demands of a transitional age.

C. S. Lewis in the **Allegory of Love** distinguishes between symbolism and allegory. He points out that if symbolism is the use of the actual to represent the reality behind it, allegory is going in the opposite direction by using fiction to represent the actual. If the narrative of the poet's pilgrimage is fictitious, the journey of his soul for which it stands is real.[46] Moreover, allegory is supposed to be the expression of a static process of thought, while a symbol, that of a dynamic process. The former sets limits to the association of ideas, the latter sets ideas in motion and keeps them rolling. As interesting as the potentialities of each might seem most

Decadents chose symbols rather than allegory. O'Sullivan is an exception in this case. Being drawn to medieval conventions and in need of expressing religious ideas he believed that allegory was more suitable for his purpose. Yet the fact that he held the inner world of man as well as an important source for his materials forced him to consider the possibilities that symbols offered.

"Mysticism is the quest for first-hand intimacy with God, the Divine, the Source, the Ground." This "direct contact with God entails the melting of the boundaries and the complete loss of one's sense of individual identity."[47] It is the dissolution of the self in an ecstatic union with the Divine. The artists of the time were deeply interested in the concept of Becoming because that represented a process, a continuous activity, which would lead to a state of Being, a state of completeness in which there is no void, a state which breaks the continuity of the relative. The artists' interest in the occult is the result of their being driven by vague spiritual desires that they display in a half-serious, half-playful manner. Generally speaking, this generation was fascinated by the element of mysticism because it transcends the tangible and physical. There is a widespread spiritualism with emphasis on Saints, the Christian rituals on a symbolic and sacramental level, on the whole, a general tendency, and an attraction to Catholicism. Conversely, there is a clear fascination with Satan and his idealization as well as an acute attraction to sin and evil. These two opposing attitudes led to an unprecedented spiritual crisis. The conflict became the hallmark of this pessimistic period. In their work artists such as O'Sullivan, conveyed effectively the paradox that was generated as a result of the central role of Satan and sin co-existing with the aesthetic and idyllic forms of Christianity. Decadence was "a form of soul-sickness, and the only cure for the disease was mysticism. But there was also another form of the soul's unrest which sprang more out of exclusive vitality strained by the hush of custom."[48] It is no wonder then that new conceptions, beliefs, lifestyles, and morality were in demand.

To know the aspects of reality which are not apparent to normal consciousness sometimes seems nonsensical to man. Man's effort to penetrate the ultimate secret of the universe and of his own nature and destiny is a mystical experience. *Theologica Mystica* is a particular type of insight and knowledge about God. Medieval *contemplatio* is a rare and advanced form of spiritual experience. To attain a state of contemplation a man has to withdraw from the world and follow a way of life entirely different from that of the world. O'Sullivan conceived of mysticism as the art of uniting with Divine Reality. It is the endeavor of the human mind to grasp the Divine essence or the ultimate reality of things and to enjoy the blessedness of actual communion with the highest. This union brings rest and peace to the soul. Saint Augustine expresses the idea when he says: "Thou hast made us for thyself, O God, and our hearts are restless till they rest in thee."[49] The moment the soul turns away from the love of transitory things that distract and destroy it and withdraws to itself, it realizes its own worth as well as the dangers which threaten it. When man meditates on the mysteries of the Divine working for the salvation of the soul, the soul finds the way to God. By contemplating truth it attains truth, and partakes through reason in the blessedness of God. But the Church's means of grace is necessary since God can only dwell in the soul that has been transformed by grace, only then can Christ, as the bridegroom, lead that soul home to Heaven and God. Withdrawal from material things, turning inward to one's own soul, and detachment eventually from one's self lead to union with God. The entry of God's light in the depths of the human soul is the aim of salvation and the meaning of Christianity. To accomplish this union with the Divine O'Sullivan had to withdraw to his inner world, and to follow the ways of Saints such as Teresa, Bonaventure, and John of the Cross. In the following chapters the reader will trace the path O'Sullivan's persona follows first to the court of heaven and then to God's embrace.

Some of the poems written at the end of the nineteenth

century deal with religious and love themes while simultaneously they represent the spirit of Victorian England. It should not be forgotten though, that faith in God and religious ideas in general, was becoming weaker, as it was in the process of being gradually abandoned. The people who found refuge in religion were desperate and oppressed intellectuals like a few Decadent poets who previously had turned to drugs and Eastern cults as an outlet against societal pressure. Needless to mention, the vast majority of them died of an overdose or committed suicide. People had started to drift away from religion and the church as early as the mid-nineteenth century that is, before these poems were written. Hugh Walker in **Literature of the Victorian Era** indicates that

> ... the Biblical chronology is abandoned; the word inspiration has wholly changed its meaning; a profound silence is observed with regard to the doctrine of eternal punishment. Bishops and dignitaries of the church pick and choose among the miracles, and invent marvelous hypotheses to reconcile the doctrine of the fall with the theory.[50]

On the contrary, the main theme in O'Sullivan's poems is that of man seeking salvation for his sins through punishment, and the rejection of his previously sinful life. Salvation was regarded as the goal of all earthly action, and divine grace the means by which it could be earned. From the religious point of view, it is "an institutionally approved means of eliminating excessive guilt stemming from the awareness of having transgressed in thought, word, or deed."[51] Undoubtedly belief in religion is a prerequisite for salvation. O'Sullivan's persona seeks God through confession of his sins and a feeling of guilt for having neglected God. However, it is noted that by the end the persona, and by definition the poet, is not confused any more. He is tranquil because he is confident that he has found the perfect means that leads out of the abyss. The way to enter God's kingdom is by admitting religion in one's heart since this is the only proven assurance against eternal damnation. Therefore whoever experiences guilt and quests for redemption attempts self-regeneration. In relation to religion some of the poets of the nineties, including O'Sullivan, dealt with the concept of death in their poems. Often the reader witnesses the persona's desire to die in a heroic attempt in order to seek God and immortality. At the same time, there is a constant endeavor to suppress flesh and exalt the spirit. The result is a fomented consciousness, a consciousness that suffers from constant guilt, frustration and disillusion. The wish for death was attuned to the religious framework of the period where "one had to hate the world, the flesh, and the devil, and keep all of God's commandments, and live as if the ties of this life were already broken."[52]

    Death became an attractive subject for study because it gave man the opportunity to acquire knowledge of the grave. But the fact that death never ceased to be an intimidating state that demanded all the courage and determination man could muster to go through it should not be overlooked. At first, the Decadents, including O'Sullivan, thought of death as an enchanting state but gradually enchantment gave in and became an obsession. Martin Heiddeger claimed that the awareness of death confers upon man a sense of his own individuality. Dying, he said is the one thing no one can do for anyone; each individual must die alone. To shut out the consciousness of death is, therefore, to refuse one's individuality it is to live inauthentically. [53] As for Saint Augustine who considered death from a religious perspective said that it is a punishment for human sin. Hence the fear of death cannot be overcome except through divine grace. Obviously the artists of the nineties who wanted to put a stamp on their sterile period could have thought of stressing their individuality by dealing with the concept of death. And as for those who were religiously inclined such as O'Sullivan Saint Augustine's view of death was an additional idea to deal with. The question many Decadents asked about death was whether it could offer a life free of sorrow, a life of eternal peace and joy, or if it was capable of leading man to rebirth and, consequently, immortality, or was it the means to eternal darkness, loss, and nothingness? Following that line of thought there was one more question that lingered in the mind of the Decadents and that was whether death was a state to desire or to shun? After all, the present life of sorrow and frustration might prove to be better than a life that death would bring along of which they knew nothing. Maybe it was better to cling to what they already had. In this light Ernest Dowson exclaims:

> Forget to-morrow!
> Weep nothing: only lay
> In silent sorrow
> Thine head my way;
> Let us forget to-morrow,
> This one day.[54]

And in his poem *Transition* Dowson says:

> A little while to hold thee and to stand,
> By harvest-fields of bending golden corn:
> Then the predestined silence, and thine hand,
> Lost in the night, long and weary and forlorn.

And at the end of the same poem the dilemma of whether to seek death or not, posed by the poet, remains unresolved. According to the Decadents a few men held fast to life, but, at the same time, continued to be haunted by the idea that death was not only inevitable but also an attractive and mysterious state.

> Short summer-time and then, my heart's desire,
> The winter and the darkness: one by one
> The roses fall, the pale roses expire
> Beneath the slow decadence of the sun.[55]

Lionel Johnson, another of O'Sullivan's contemporaries, describes the attraction that death had for him in *The Last Music*. The poet begins by an invitation to the maids to play music fit for his "dead queen." As the poem proceeds the reader realizes that the dead queen continues to represent beauty and that death has not changed her appearance nor did it mar her beauty. To this effect the poet says: "she lies / Dead: and more beautiful."[56] The poet conveys the impression that death has the potential to freeze beauty forever and as such beauty is to be found not only in life but also in death. Hence, as perverse as it may sound, it was considered normal for the poets of the nineties to assume that a man enamored with beauty was simultaneously charmed and lured by death. Consequently, for the Decadents the state of death is a state of beauty, a state deeply desired yet feared. As Johnson confirms:

> The balm of gracious death now laps her round,
> As once life gave her grace beyond her peers.
> Strange! that I loved this lady of the spheres,
> To sleep by her at last in common ground:
> When kindly sleep hath bound
> Mine eyes, and sealed mine ears.[57]

According to these poets whoever experienced death acquired the ability to enjoy beauty, which was believed to be the center of their life. Furthermore, whoever experienced death also meant that he would attain the desired state of peace, either religiously or psychologically. Hence any complications man's life had would be obliterated and it would eventually become bearable. As such death and beauty became the ideal combination. What else could man wish for? The peace that death brings from the turmoil of life is vividly depicted in Johnson's poem *Nihilism*.

> Only the rest! Only the gloom,
> Soft and long gloom! the pausing from all
>   thought!
> My life, I cannot taste: the eternal tomb
> Brings me the peace, which life has never
>   brought.[58]

Only the "slow approach of perfect death" can offer him peace and joy, feelings that have proven non-existent in life.

John Davidson, another Decadent poet, describes the fate of man in his poem *The Price* by saying that somehow man was born to stay for a short while on earth before death comes along to sweep him away. Fate's grand design is for man's wellbeing only that he does not know it, and needs to discover it. Life and death seem to be man's lot and he is obviously powerless to change that. The very knowledge that death is around the corner, "loading dice," makes it impossible for man to live in peace. "A blossom once or twice, / Love lights on Summer's hearth; / But Winter loads the dice." And again "the dance is done in a trice; / Death belts his bony girth; / And struts, and rattles his dice."[59] So, according to Davidson, man cannot escape from life on earth as he cannot escape from death. The poet conveys the idea of man's weakness in the face of his fate, or God's design about him.

Finally, in Arthur Symons' poem *Epilogue: Credo* the poet introduces the theme of the *carpe diem* in connection with death. Symons intended to draw attention to the fact that the so-called desired state of death might have nothing to offer after all, and that man should think about that possibility as well before deciding to choose death. Symons, like Pater, Wilde, and so many other Decadents, believed that man should lead a full life on earth. He says:

> For of our time we lose so large a part
> In serious trifles, and so oft let slip
> The wine of every moment, at the lip
> Its moment, and the moment of the heart.

And in the last stanza the poet expresses his doubt of an after-life, a doubt that should prompt man to seize the moment and make the most of it because after death there is certainly no sign that life exists.

> We are awake so little on the earth,
> And we shall sleep so long, and rise so late,
> If there is any knocking at that gate

Which is the gate of death, the gate of birth.[60]

And even though there is so much talk about death's ability to bring about regeneration still man has no guarantees that that is what he is to expect to happen after death. Hence there seems to be no other alternative but to choose to "burn with that gemlike flame" which according to Pater is life's objective.[61]

The concept of death as O'Sullivan conveys it is obviously an experience that takes the soul into another dimension of reality, a reality that is completely unknown to the soul before death. The experience of death is described as a dark space, a cave, a void, a vacuum which, once inside, the soul discovers it is full of concentric circles which it has to follow, and as it does, it transports itself gradually higher and higher. As the process continues and the soul moves onward man sees more and more light and becomes aware of the limitations of his body, this is a sign that the soul is moving upward. Gradually death becomes the release, the escape from the prison of the flesh. According to Plato the soul comes into the body from a higher and more divine realm of existence. Therefore death is a sleep and a forgetting through which the soul goes back to its pre-natal state, the state of consciousness and knowledge. The poet borrowed the idea from William Wordsworth who dealt with it in his *Intimations to Immortality: An Ode* at the beginning of the nineteenth century. During the period of transition from the one state to the other man achieves wisdom because this is the time when his reason is able to function at its best and it can recognize the true nature of things as never before. O'Sullivan added to his concept of death his biblical knowledge when he refers to Judgment Day and the return of the Lord. There will be a general resurrection of the dead, where the bodies we lost in death will be given back to us and we will become again whole. Only Paradise and Hell will remain, Purgatory will disappear because it will have no function. At last, the body will be subject to the spirit and free from suffering, corruption, and all the natural necessities of earthly life. In addition, the body will be endowed with a supernatural beauty and eminence since it will share in the glory of the soul. There will be no more change, no principle of time, but only eternity. Perfect happiness consists in forgetting oneself, in living not for oneself, but solely for God, giving oneself to Him, losing oneself in Him, living only to love Him, to adore Him, to give Him the glory that is His due.

O'Sullivan like most of his contemporaries willingly accepted the fact that the Victorian period was neurotic because, as Masao Miyoshi says in ***The Divided Self: A Perspective on the Literature of the Victorians,*** "neurosis is lapsing in non-being hence losing autonomy, life, reality, identity."[62] The Victorians conformed to the prevalent patterns of behavior without asking any questions. On the contrary, the Decadents could not bring themselves to accept the very idea of conformity so they were faced with no other choice but to rebel. In the meantime, they hoped to overcome this so-called neurosis by behaving differently and establishing a new reality, attaining a new identity, and putting, in this way, their mark on the Victorian age.

O'Sullivan deemed the philosophical and religious frameworks that supported the Victorian age inadequate. This realization compelled him to create his own myth. He turned to the traditional quest romance and chose to internalize it. As the poet's quest unravels, multiple personae emerge that act as masks of the poet and various myths of the soul take shape. By means of these masks O'Sullivan avoided sinking into autobiographical writing and synchronously achieved objectivity. Yet it should be remembered that the nature of the poet's subject remains highly personal. As a result, dealing with the weakness of the human soul implies confronting the weakness of his soul as well. In addition, the poet used these masks not only to project the many stages the human soul goes through in its mystical quest, but also to delineate step by step the discovery of his identity as well as the process of his development as an individual and as a thinker.

O'Sullivan's poetry is the product of an intellect

concerned with religious and metaphysical subjects. One of the dominant themes is that of the soul's fragility in resisting sin and temptation. One witnesses the poet's effort to find suitable ways to save man's soul as well as his. Every man, says the poet, has to be strong and resolute when it comes to making a decision to change his lifestyle. Actually, throughout his poetry the feeling that there is no time to lose or room for vacillation is successfully conveyed. Fear of punishment and eternal suffering in Hell urges him to abandon his old ways and move forward in search of salvation. Evidently the religious ideas of sin, punishment, and redemption preoccupied O'Sullivan, as many other *fin-de-siècle* artists, because, in his opinion, they formed an essential part of man's spiritual being.

In **Aspects of Wilde** O'Sullivan says that Oscar Wilde was not a great poet because he had no "interior life."

> By this is meant that condition in which men and women have colloquies with their soul and take knowledge of it; are impelled to prayer and to contact with the prime forces of our being; come to secret terms with their passions either to satisfy or to suppress them. It is the condition usually ascribed to some form of religion and Teresa of Avila, the Spanish nun of the sixteenth century, is as good an example as any of the interior life developed by religion.[63]

In each man there is a true self that does not change with bodily or mental transformations, with the flux of sensations, with the dissipation of ideas, or with the fading of memories. The true self is immortal, constant, and unchanging, and is not bound by space or time because it is divine. In Christian mysticism it is the spark, the center or the apex of the soul, or the ground of the spirit. According to John of Ruysbroeck the "third property of the soul is called the spark of the soul."[64] It is the inward and natural tendency of the soul toward its source. Through it man receives the Holy Spirit, the utmost charity of God to him. With the "inward tendency" man becomes one with the spirit of God. Meister Eckhart describes the process when he says, "the power of the Holy Ghost seizes the very brightest and purest, the spark of the soul, and carries it up in the flame of love... the soul spark is conveyed aloft into its source and is absorbed into God and is identified with God and is the spiritual light of GOD."[65] The spark as such is what "the soul uses to have communion with God and know HIM, it is the essence of the Being and Nature of God Himself" in man.[66]

The poems O'Sullivan wrote can be considered as personal expressions, confessions, or semi-biographical records. But they can also be regarded as the entries of a journal through which the reader witnesses the rake's progress from vice to virtue. The sinner is seen turning away from the common woman, who brought up in him the passion of lust, to the Holy Virgin who fills his heart with spiritual and religious ecstasy. Finally, the reader is given the opportunity to discern the poet's mind in motion as it creates situations in which the persona adopts the pose of the ardent lover languishing in expectation for the day when his soul will unite with his beloved/Christ.

O'Sullivan's poetry abounds with references to the beloved, the temptress, and the repentant fallen woman, or femme fatale. Theologians point out, that woman in the Bible is sometimes described as good and so is taken to be symbolic of the church. Yet at some other point in history she was viewed as evil and as representative of the lower or weaker side of man, his carnal desires or lust, as well as his mutable mind. In addition, because woman tends to tempt with her beauty she was identified with deceit. The poet used these two sets of contradictory ideas to construct a psychological as well as theological framework for his poems. In his poetry, O'Sullivan implies that when love awakens man to a new awareness of himself, he is expected to turn to God, but unfortunately woman draws him instead to worldly desire. In some contexts he shows that whenever man succeeds in overcoming his lower impulses a union with the woman he loves is possible. That union is significant because it yields harmony within and facilitates his relationships in the world he lives in. This union assumes a psychological dimension as well since it alludes to the internal conflict between the opposing principles: male and female that underline man's being. When conflict, temporarily or lastingly ceases, peace prevails.

According to Joan Ferrente, whenever the theme of love is dominant in lyric poetry and mystical writings woman is presented as a force of good. Thus woman is seen as an independent individual who has the potential to act and bring about change. In this light "woman is no longer a symbol of something in man; she becomes a separate entity, an angel, a star, or the Virgin Mary."[67] Furthermore, woman acquires an additional function, she becomes an intermediary between man and God, and man's goal is not to unite with her, but rather to use her to achieve a union with the Divine. The Virgin is portrayed in medieval art as the throne of wisdom and Christ on her lap stands for that wisdom. This is a perfect example of the harmony that results when male and female figures unite. The contempt for women is expressed by using the story of Eve's sin. This idea of the inferior and seductive female changed only because of the Holy Virgin's role. Through time the devotion to Mary served, at least partly, to counterbalance the negative view of woman. After all, it was the life of Mary that made the redemption of the human race possible.

Through her beauty woman has the power to seduce man away from his purpose as well as to draw him away from spirit and intellect to matter. It is the lower impulses of man that give in to a woman's temptations; these impulses man has to learn to control, and not reject. According to Carl Jung's theory man is *spiritus*, rational soul, and woman is the *anima*, the lower soul.[68] She is considered responsible for throwing man from grace since he is vulnerable to her wiles. In this context the metaphor of marriage is supposed to bring together the two in a harmonious relationship. Moreover, in the Bible, Eve is a part of Adam having been created from his side. This means that man and woman have to learn to integrate. From the psychological point of view, the male and female principles have to coexist in concord. But there is a religious significance to this union as well since without it a union with the Divine, which is, and should remain, the ultimate goal in every man's life is impossible. This point of view yields woman a positive role to play in the moral development of man, a role given to her by God since He created her to complement Adam. At the same time, if man insists on blaming woman, or accusing her for his failure, he is abdicating his own role as a man.

The allegorical tradition in literature presents a number of important concepts. One of them is the union of the opposites as the basic principle of life. It is evident that there is a need for the female to stand alongside the male if harmony and completion are to be attained. The idea that woman is identified with good qualities and not only with evil forces is significant because, in this way, woman attains an additional role. Consequently, once she ceases to be seen as a temptress, she is cast as man's good angel that has the potential to lead him upward. O'Sullivan uses this dual view of woman as the analysis of his poetry, that will ensue in the following two chapters, will show. Moreover, the woman the persona is in love with is symbolically depicted as a mirror in which he sees his soul as it should be and not as it is. In the process the poet outlines the soul's drama as it embattles ardently and constantly the lower impulses. In this context the woman projected has a double function since she is a helping figure as well as an obstructing one.[69] Finally, woman is also seen as an active force in man's spiritual drama as the persona's prayers to the Virgin Mary exemplify.

O'Sullivan deals primarily with religious themes in his poetry. In a number of poems he refers to a beloved whose identity is never revealed, and who might be only a figment of his imagination. Even though the woman he describes is illiterate, licentious, unfaithful, and seductive, she somehow is the source of his inspiration. Thus many poems that suggest sensuality never deal with the fulfillment of desire. The impression the writer conveys is that the persona is content just to look at the woman who excites him, sometimes, even dream of her, without ever meeting her once. As such physical pleasure is only the product of the imagination and remains throughout his poetry intangible, and a fantasy. At the same time, together with the sensual there is a powerful religious force that springs from within and that compels the persona to restrain from pleasure. The question that arises in the reader's mind is whether O'Sullivan assumed sensuality as a pose in order to impress his readers while deep down in his heart he was uneasy about every sin he delineated? The answer is yes, because the poet followed what was common practice with many writers of the *fin-de-siècle*. Therefore, on the one hand, an obstinate insistence on sin resulting in feelings of distress can be detected in his poetry. The poet juxtaposes the insistence and attraction of sin with the acknowledgment that sin is the devil's creation that merits punishment. On the other hand, the ideal world that is spiritual and immortal, a world that cannot be ignored, a world after which man aspires because it is beautiful and pure is continuously stressed. It goes without saying that the conflict between the sensual and the spiritual results constantly in torment and suffering. Yet this type of suffering per se seems to be enjoyed and glorified. Actually the longer the pain lasts and the harsher it is the more likely it is believed to lead to redemption. Finally, O'Sullivan believed that even though sin and despair were prevalent, the Ideal was still more powerful and vivid and remained a part of man's aspiration toward eternity, a part of man's yearning that cannot be overlooked. In this way no one can ignore the intensity of his desire to unite with the Divine.

In O'Sullivan's poetry the religious themes are conveyed in a secular diction. Evidently he does not opt for a Platonic relationship, instead he transforms the Platonic into a springboard from where he can attain a more valuable relationship with the Virgin Mary and Jesus. Life is man's God given chance to travel and when the journey ends he will find himself where he began, that is, at the beginning. In other words, man is bound to return to his Mother, to the earth, through death and hence to the starting point that is, heaven, even if the journey takes him a lifetime. But the journey of life, as O'Sullivan has shown in his poetry, is filled with numberless hardships and tribulations.

What O'Sullivan is seeking is more than just physical beauty or virtue of the mind he is definitely seeking for a lasting union with the Divine. So that his love poems and his impassioned expressions are not for a specific woman, but for the only Woman/Mother in whose embrace he feels safe from the world. That seems to be the ultimate pleasure, a spiritual sort of pleasure that resembles John Donne's "ecstasy" where the soul is seen moving freely outside the body.[70] A state where to die means to live, and to lose to find a new consciousness. O'Sullivan's poetry begins with the expression of simple physical experiences that intensify as they change and become spiritual and mystical. The experience that starts in the form of a voyage will hopefully end in a Holy marriage. The journey is about man's soul encountering Holy love after transformation, through grace, occurs and before uniting with the Divine. The quest leads from the abyss of Hell to the zenith of Heaven, from total darkness to blinding light, from despair to hope, from the sensuality of the physical to the spirituality of the holy and the union with the Divine, from mortality to immortality. The journey takes the soul from the limitations of time to a state of timelessness and a different state of reality. Consequently, the voyage depicted in which the persona progresses does not follow a horizontal line only, but spirals upward since the journey changes direction after a while. First the persona learns to walk away from the world of sensuality, and physicality, and that is when he travels horizontally. Gradually, and after the process of cleansing sets in, the persona is seen climbing a ladder up to heaven and that is when the direction of his progress shifts upward. It is at this stage that the persona is seen slowly detaching himself from his physical surroundings and attempting an emotional relationship with the Holy Virgin and Christ. Everything around him that is supposed to be associated with physical reality becomes part of death and only this new relationship with the Holy Mother and her Son fills him with life. Naturally, part of O'Sullivan's poetry deals with the distinctions he draws between the finite and the infinite, the actual and the ideal states that are experienced by his persona.

Deep within each individual there is an amazing "sanctuary of the soul" a holy place, a Divine Center, a speaking Voice, to which one may continuously return. There is no doubt that eternity exists deep in every heart, it is known to press upon every one's time-ravaged life, "warning us with intimations of amazing destiny, calling us home unto itself." Beginning to yield to these persuasions, gladly committing both body and soul, utterly and completely, to the light within, is the beginning of true life. This Divine center is a creative life that presses to be born within each one. That inward light is eternal, it "never fades, but burns, a perpetual flame."[71] It becomes the most faithful guide of one's life, and has the potential to expose a few of one's unsuspected defects as well as those of one's fellow men.

O'Sullivan's poetry presents his determination to seek and find his lost soul. To express this idea successfully and objectively O'Sullivan created a persona who first projects his soul and then confronts it. The confrontation renders the dialogue that takes place between the persona and his soul concrete. Rarely by the use of symbols, and more often through images, the poet makes the reader accept the idea that the persona's soul is actually lost and he has to do all in his capacity to save it. It should be borne in mind that throughout his poetry O'Sullivan identifies with his persona and consequently makes the tormenting experience of the persona his own. Therefore, it is the poet's soul that the reader sees submerging in the spiritual apathy of Victorian England. In an attempt to rejuvenate his soul the poet creates the persona, a double, with which he seeks integration before a complete individual emerges. Like most *fin-de-siècle* writers O'Sullivan felt bewildered and confused, so he decided to join his persona on the long mystical journey, achieve knowledge of his true self, and recover his soul. Actually, what he wished to do was to save his soul from the ashes of Victorian conformity. To describe convincingly this spiritual inward journey he adopted medieval conventions, mythic patterns, and the structure of the quest. In his opinion, this was the most apt method of objectifying an intense personal drama. As a matter of fact, this method proved successful in turning an exclusively private experience into a universal one.

Rollo May says: "that we experience ourselves as a thinking-intuiting-feeling and acting unity. Thyself is thus not merely the sum of the various roles one plays; it is the center from which one sees and is aware of these so-called different sides of himself."[72] Similarly, one can say that a number of roles spring from within, roles that help man in his long journey toward Heaven. Through these roles the persona moves from one situation to another gaining not only knowledge but also the strength to resist sin and consequently start the process of purification.

What does it mean to experience one's self as a self? The experience of one's identity is basic for one's psychological being. It can never be proven in a logical sense, for consciousness of one's self is the presupposition of any discussion about it. There will always be an element of mystery in one's awareness of one's own being. For such awareness is a prerequisite of inquiry into one's self and means that one is already engaging in self-consciousness.[73] But to know one's self is to find one's lost soul for without it man is incomplete as an individual and as a self. Finding one's soul is a spiritual process that parallels the psychological process of finding one's self. The soul is heavenly while the self is worldly, and man needs both to be first complete and then content.

O'Sullivan adopted the Romantic view that considered the poet a hero and a prophet. In the Romantic tradition the poet possesses knowledge and is given a grandiose stature since he is compared to the oracle that conveyed its message of the universe to ordinary man. The Decadent artist did not believe, as his Victorian contemporary, that he had to devote his artistic powers in the interest of society, or that he had to be society's moral guide or spiritual counselor. Instead, the Decadent chose the romantic mode in order to expose his personal experience. He believed that presenting his experience and letting it speak was more evocative. Yet some Decadents agreed with the Aesthetes who professed that art had the power to redeem society and make the world a better place for man to live in. In this light some artists used their art to expose social problems and offer possible solutions. In the case of O'Sullivan, the reader notices a combination of ideas borrowed from John Ruskin who attached a social function to art, and Robert Browning who argued that art is a manifestation of the Divine that expresses itself through the artist's imagination. In addition, even though O'Sullivan is not considered a fervent aesthete like Pater or Wilde, still he borrowed many of their concepts, and, varied them to suit his ideas. Actually, O'Sullivan can be considered more of a romantic because he is introspective and confessional in his poetry. For example, he denounced the hedonistic philosophy that Pater propounded and which prevailed in an age where the old moral values were fast crumbling. Throughout his poetry O'Sullivan not only belittles the power of the physical and the sensual, but he also extols the spiritual. Furthermore, he counteracts the philosophy of Pater and the Aesthetes by introducing the idea that man has to wrench all sensual pleasures from his life. According to O'Sullivan man has to learn to live intensely not in the sensual manner but in the ascetic manner by following a spiritual way of life. Pater stressed the sensations and sense impressions in association with beauty, which he considered the ultimate objective in man's life. On the contrary, O'Sullivan focused on religious beauty therefore the adoration of the Virgin Mary and her Child is the ultimate vision of beauty. And as for the union with the Divine that, is considered the most important experience in man's life. Profane experience is for the aesthete the subject matter for unique art while for O'Sullivan it is religious and metaphysical experience. That view echoes more medieval artistic practice than *fin-de-siècle* sensuous aesthetics. Finally, by imitating the aesthetes, O'Sullivan explored the mystery of human consciousness and colored it by his own religiosity.

O'Sullivan followed Medieval and Renaissance writers who used medieval conventions such as allegory to depict Truth. Unlike Edmund Spenser, who used allegory to describe a Platonic ideal, O'Sullivan was keen on conveying religious truth, the sort of truth on which man's salvation depends. After a long investigation he concluded that the kind of truth that would be useful to man is factual and less doctrinal. Yet truth had to be achieved by a long and painful process of search and not by a sudden beatific vision as many Medieval artists claimed. Given the fact that man has to look hard for the truth, the question that recurs is where is he supposed to look for it? But no matter the effort he is to exert and the time he is to spend, he should persist because down deep in his heart he knows that if he does not find it he will live forever in the insufferable abyss. Normally without action there is no realization, and a truth which does not emerge in life after actively searching for it is a truth which lacks efficacy. Last but not least, it should be pointed out that there is no doubt that truth is an inner state which unfolds the meaning of everything that happens, everything that touches one's life. Thus the discovery of the nature of truth is an uncovering of what exists within.

Northrop Frye says that "the hero of the internalized quest is the poet himself, and the antagonists he encounters on his quest are those other parts of his self that keep blocking the imagination." He goes on to say that the fulfillment is never the actual poem itself, but the poem beyond that is made possible by the apocalypse of the imagination."[74] Moreover, Frye points out that the direction of the quest for identity is bound to lead increasingly downward and inward "toward a hidden basis or ground of identity between man and nature." A unity which is impossible if transformation of both man and nature is not accomplished.[75] The direction which is downward and inward is supposedly common for every individual and that is the one O'Sullivan adopts in order to achieve that inner union with the Divine. O'Sullivan's persona hearkens to the call and once he accepts it he descends into the underworld where he goes through a series of trials. After the fulfillment of the quest he returns apotheosized by the sacred marriage, which in O'Sullivan takes place between the persona's soul and the Divine. When the persona returns he ceases to be an individual and becomes an eternal timeless figure, some sort of a prophet with a mission in the world: to teach and share with mankind the wisdom he has obtained. O'Sullivan's persona, who attains the desired union with the Divine, returns to earth to save and help other tormented souls. In this light the poet does not suggest simply to teach but also to guide whoever reads his poetry in the same manner his persona guides lost souls out of the abyss to Heaven.

Death is an essential part of the spiritual process and the quest. As a matter of fact, it is a basic aspect of the experience because rebirth can be achieved only through death. The impulse toward renewal, restoration, or rejuvenation is present in O'Sullivan's poetry. The metaphor is religious and mythic simultaneously. The journey toward the Divine is regarded in terms of the soul's renewal, as purification and immortality are granted in the process. In so far as the journey is undertaken for the expiation of guilt it involves death, since what is sought is the renewal of a former state of innocence.[76]

The entire collection of **Poems** reads like one long allegorical poem where a hero is seen taking a quest. Whereas in the romance the knight quests for the Holy Grail O'Sullivan's persona quests for the ultimate union with the Divine, thus bringing inner peace and harmony, and most of all, relief from torture. As for the second collection, **The Houses of Sin,** it plunges the reader into the medieval world and its philosophy by using the concept of the seven deadly sins. O' Sullivan thought he could escape from the world of the *fin de siècle*, a world of broken images and incoherent ideas, a world of confusion, distress, and pain by retreating in time. The religiosity of the medieval age helped him understand the fall of man and fathom the implications of the fallen condition. Like so many of his contemporaries who looked for ways of evasion, O'Sullivan found that escape in the medieval world with its religion, romance, and allegory. Unquestionably the medieval world possessed a religious mystique for it provided him with the desired flight that successfully took him out of his present inferno. So when he decided to start his first collection with an address to the soul and conclude it with the futility of the body that will turn to dust, he actually conveyed the main idea that came to underline his philosophy of life. Furthermore, the idea that the world he lived in was as ugly and hectic as Hell as a result of the fall is also imparted. Deeply dissatisfied with the Victorian world as he was, it is no wonder that he yearned to leave it behind and embark on a quest to discover the spiritual world.

Many of O'Sullivan's poems resemble short dramas that start *in medias res*. They provide vivid settings with colorful objects. In the poems there is always a listener who is no other than the poet, and by identification the reader, and who is willing to listen to everything the speaker, in this case, the persona, says. The persona is seen addressing his soul and exposing his innermost thoughts and feelings. Needless to mention that the dialogue, a method the poet chooses, takes place between the soul which has been first projected, making it in this way an independent entity, and the persona who addresses it. Frequently, the persona reveals that he has had a sinful past that impinges on his present. It is a past he wishes to leave behind and free himself from it completely. Often O'Sullivan exposes every detail of the situations he creates in which he describes the existence of a triangular relationship among the persona and his projected body/lover as well as his soul/beloved in full enactment. To these situations he usually adds speech turning them into dramatic monologues wherein the feelings of past innocence and present sinfulness are outlined by the persona.

In ***A Study of English Romanticism*** Frye argues that the heroic quest that takes the hero from darkness to light is "a dialectical one." It is "a passage not from death to life only, but a transformation to a new and timeless life which takes the form of an ascending spiral which does not end before it arrives at the highest point of light and awareness."[77] Hence transformation and the passage seem to be identical once they are completed and the soul is in the embrace of the Divine forever. From the psychological point of view, the basic theme of entrapment and liberation as an inner process of creating the self through projection, fragmentation, and integration is also conveyed. Finally, the reader realizes the active interaction between the basic instincts of life and death which underline each man's consciousness.

Man is a sharer in the Divine life and he longs to return to that from which he feels he has come. Simultaneously he yearns to be more closely and consciously linked with the Divine. He feels he is a pilgrim of eternity and a creature of time, yet a citizen of a timeless world. Even though he clings to selfhood and self-love, he still wishes to unite with something eternal, beautiful, and inexplicable to which he feels he belonged and from which he has been separated by birth. Only in mystical experience the dilemma of duality which preoccupies and tortures man is resolved. For the mystic is given that unifying vision of the One is All and the All is One.[78] All feelings of duality and multiplicity are obliterated, including the duality between man and Deity. Hence man recognizes the timelessness of his experience. Every soul that departs in grace goes to Heaven or ends there after cleansing itself. Heaven is envisioned as a place of perfect happiness. It is the end of the journey. It is the place where the soul is fully satisfied because it possesses God as well as infinite Good. O'Sullivan stresses, in his poetry, the idea that man "gropes in the dark, but there are always gleams of light that come from God. The only possible answer to the problem of man's destiny is to seek without respite to fulfill God's purpose. And man should allow himself to be guided."[79]

O'Sullivan's poems can easily be characterized as metaphysical since they express dialectically a personal drama. His poetry is based on the principle of man's relationship to God. It is the treatment of this principle that echoes a number of metaphysical poets such as George Herbert, Richard Crashaw, and Henry Vaughan. As is the case with the expression of a metaphysical experience sometimes the images and analogies may seem far-fetched. But it should be noted that what lies in the soul of man cannot be expressed simply by following a sequential method. O'Sullivan's poetry is a sample of the self and soul at work. After all, isolated instances of spiritual or mystical experience can make sense only on the basis of their own logic. Instead of using complex conceits as John Donne did in order to yoke "the most heterogeneous ideas...by violence," O'Sullivan chose simple medieval conventions to convey his metaphysical experiences.[80] Readers found the fusion of the metaphysical content with the psychological intent, new and interesting. It is the successful utilization of conventions that helped him turn his personal experience into impersonal. Most of his poetry is based on real or imaginary dramatic situations in which often paradoxical and contradictory elements are presented in action. An example of that is his poem *Rivals*. The dramatic situations he creates in order to convey his mystical experience make his poetry very similar to that of the metaphysical poets. But even though the emotion evoked is overwhelming still his poetry is characterized by simplicity. As for the ideas, they are exposed in a manner that makes them easy to grasp. It is the sort of poetry that can touch anybody who reads it because everyone has experienced, at least once, the same qualms about one's sinful condition and some have undergone a similar mystical experience.

O'Sullivan agrees with Bonaventure's concept of the mystical journey being a mental one. Normally one searches for God by His traces in the external world. Surely enough, though, one can find Him only within. Thus Bonaventure says man contemplates God "outside through His traces, inside through His image, and above through His light which has signed upon our minds the light of eternal Truth."[81] It is noteworthy that the individual who decides to take the quest has to deal with both his self as well as his soul, for God exists in both. God exists in Heaven and on earth, and if man can detect His presence on earth then he can unite with Him in Heaven. Moreover, if man can find the image of God in his soul then he can also achieve an everlasting union between his soul and God.

Hardest of all for O'Sullivan's persona was his conviction that he had already abused God's mercy and squandered His gifts. Such moments of realization led him to periods of relapse, or spiritual dryness when he could see nothing but darkness without and emptiness within. During that time he believed he had no right to ask for illumination or God's grace and guidance. But all the same, he was constantly reminded of God's boundless charity and love. He never forgot that he could pray for God's help if he decided to set out on his journey. Moreover, he pleaded for the clouds to dissolve and the mist to lift so that his way to the land of light may be clearly mapped and the journey simplified. These feelings, O'Sullivan suggested, are familiar to any man who decides to set out on such a crucial, yet meaningful quest.

Sin cuts off man from God. It brings inevitable separation, and this separation translates into spiritual death. It is the severance of a person from God that moves man from life and consequently, from light to darkness. Furthermore, man's sins blot out God's image in his soul. Until his sins are forgiven man remains an exile from his true home, which in this context is no other but Heaven where he can reside near his Father. And that is not all, because man becomes enslaved to his own earthiness that leads to a continuous corruption of his nature. Through Jesus man can come out of exile and reconcile with God, he can be reborn, and set free from his mortal bondage. In the meantime, all discord can be replaced by the harmony of love. Christ with his death on the cross liberated man from self-centeredness and brought him into harmony with his fellow men. It is true that a long time elapses before man discovers his self, but when he does, he realizes that he has to give it up because it is part of his earthly being. He acquires a new goal and that is no other but finding his soul since without it he cannot obtain salvation or the desired union with God.

"The kingdom of God is within you" (*Luke* 21). All man has to do is turn with all his heart to the Lord and forsake this "wretched world" and ultimately find peace. He has to learn to despise material things and to concentrate on things which are spiritual then "Christ will come unto thee, and show thee His own consolation, if thou prepare for Him a worthy mansion within thee." No one has to forget that "all His glory and beauty is from within." Man has to prepare his soul for the "Bridegroom that He may vouchsafe to come unto thee, and to dwell within."[82] Finally, the soul that can hear the Lord speaking within is blessed, and "receiveth from His mouth the word of consolation."[83] O'Sullivan intended to explore extensively the inner state, since he had already concluded that salvation could be achieved only by taking the mystical quest.

O'Sullivan examines the concepts of Heaven and Hell and tries to explain them through the debates he presents on sin. Hell is the place where the soul is cut off forever from God. As long as the soul is in this world it finds some happiness in the senses and whatever is associated with them. But after death the soul is transported to another level of existence where it is obliged to leave all material pleasures behind. At that time it finds itself in a vast desert where nothing satisfies it. It is driven back on itself with no relief from loneliness. Eventually, it realizes that self-indulgence, pride, carelessness, and worldliness lead to a state of torture, that is no other but Hell. To avoid the state of Hell man must try hard to attain God's grace while he is still in this life.

As for Purgatory, O'Sullivan viewed it as a place or state were souls that are saved, but not yet fit for final union with the Divine pause to rest and affirm their determination to continue the process of purification no matter how difficult that process may prove. Apparently mere admission of repentance is not enough since only suffering can cleanse the soul from the taint of sin. Before the soul is fit to enter the presence of God, all stains must be removed. Therefore one of the reasons that makes the soul accept suffering is its strong desire to return to God. Also the soul begins to recollect how radiant it was at the beginning; then, it enumerates the sins it has committed to offend God; and finally, it realizes how horrible and vile its sins are. At this moment the soul feels the burden of its sins and in order to relieve itself it decides to repent. O'Sullivan argues that paradoxically the soul continues to feel moments of happiness no matter how sinful it is because the love of God never disappears from his soul completely. In other words, God never abandons man even though man turns away from this innate and generous love. As the soul starts going through the state of purification it becomes conscious of this love. While undergoing the process of purgation the soul identifies with Christ's Passion and gradually becomes aware that its salvation is assured by the Lord's sacrifice. Hope returns slowly every day as the soul regains its ability to see a little clearer the light of God, and the realization that the day when it will be able to see God's face again is not far away. Purgatory is the place or the state which man should keenly seek so as to avoid the suffering of Hell. Furthermore, Purgatory is simply the place where man's soul will be purified and prepared for the union with the Divine. From the psychological point of view, Purgatory translates into the place where the process of self-integration is achieved and a sense of fulfillment and wholeness is experienced for the first time.

Finally, O'Sullivan assumed that if the soul arrived to Purgatory successfully then Heaven could not be far away. It seems that the hardest part of the journey is arriving to Purgatory. Once this has been attained the distance to Heaven is significantly reduced. As a matter of fact, the light of God appears slightly and participates in leading the soul to God's court. The inward light which John Milton defined in **Paradise Lost** is the same light O'Sullivan refers to.[84] This is the light of the Holy Ghost given by God to man. It is the light that can lead him to discover and regain Paradise by uncovering and developing these inner forms of truth and goodness. For O'Sullivan the inward and spiritual states is all that essentially mattered. Clearly to him Heaven and Hell are mental states which form the inner world of every man. To sin is to obscure the inward light and fall into despair and consequently death. To discover that inward light is to liberate oneself from darkness and death, it meant rebirth, that for him was the aim of life. To fully understand the reasons that prompted Vincent O'Sullivan to withdraw from the world and to turn within, one has to attempt to analyze the collapsing Victorian world in which he lived and which he, like so many writers of the *fin-de-siècle*, described as the abyss or Hell.

In conclusion, it should be pointed out that Vincent O'Sullivan, like his contemporaries, was not only puzzled by Victorian reality he also questioned it. Like his contemporaries he, too, wanted to escape the world he lived in but found it very hard to step outside it completely. Is it worth creating another world when everything is so futile, and everything is bound to turn "ashes to ashes, and dust to dust?"[84] Is it worth striving for a better world when everything is bound to turn to dust? Unlike the Decadents, it seems that the Victorians were never preoccupied by that question no wonder then they were so complacent. In his poetry O'Sullivan conveys the insoluble problems man faced in a melancholic tone. Throughout his poetry the poet does not offer any signs of optimism for a better life on earth since he was convinced that a better life was possible only if man followed in the tracks of his persona. Since there is no freedom from pain on earth, maybe then spiritual freedom has to be sought intensely, and, hopefully, it would not prove just another illusion. Like everyone else he was "wavering among institutions, ignorance, half-truths, shadows of falsehood, and new audiences. And like everyone else "hesitating he was blown hither and thither by conflicting minds, a prey to the indefinite."[85] What would happen if he were to turn to what lay inside and were to examine the various psychological urges that underlined his very being? Would that approach lead him to happiness or offer him, at least, peace? The two volumes of poems O'Sullivan wrote make use of the same persona. He identifies with his persona in order to depict his tormented soul in its quest for a new state devoid of despair and anguish. His poems embody the spirit of the age as well as the painful life of his contemporaries. It is not an exaggeration to say that O'Sullivan succeeded in describing the inconsistencies of the *fin-de-siècle* as well as his own frustrations very effectively.

    The next two chapters deal with the two volumes of poems in detail. As has already been stated the most appropriate method that leads to understanding O'Sullivan's vision is to analyze each poem individually and in the order O'Sullivan placed it in the given volume. For each one of his volumes O'Sullivan chose the specific framework of the journey. Within that structure the poet builds up tension to a peak and provides a release at the end in exactly the same manner as a dramatist would. As a result the reader finds it easy to identify with the persona and undertake the mystical journey with him. The poet fervently believed that by tracing the persona/sinner's soul in its quest from the abyss of Hell to the court of Heaven, and finally, to God's embrace the reader is bound to acquire enough knowledge to free himself from his own bondage.

NOTES
Chapter I

[1] Vincent O'Sullivan (1868-1940) was a poet, short-story writer, novelist, and essayist. He was born in New York City in 1868. He attended Oscott and then Exeter College, Oxford, but was interested more in the creation of Literature than in its study. He published *Poems* in 1896, *The Houses of Sin* in 1897, *A Book of Bargains* 1896, *The Good Girl* 1912, a translation of Louis Bertrand's *Saint Augustine* 1913, and *Aspects of Wilde* 1936.

[2] Holbrock Jackson, *The Eighteen Nineties: A Review of Art and Ideas at the Close of the Nineteenth Century* (New York: Alfred A. Knopf, 1922) 55.

[3] H. Stuart Hughes, *Consciousness and Society* (London: Paladin, 1974) 150.

[4] Winfred Baumgart, *Imperialism: The Idea and Reality of British and French Colonial Expansion 1880-1914* (Oxford: Oxford University Press, 1982) 1.

[5] Max Nordeau, *Degeneration* (New York: D. Appleton & Co., 1895) 36.

[6] Jackson, *Eighteen Nineties* 18.

[7] Jackson, 26.

[8] Estelle Lauter and Carol Schreier eds., *Feminist Archetypal Theory: Interdisciplinary Revisions of Jungian Thought* (Knoxville: University of Tennessee Press, 1985) 105.

[9] Thomas Carlyle, *Sartor Resartus* (New York: Holt, Rinehart, & Winston, 1970) 150.

[10] Carlyle, 150.

[11] Nordeau, *Degeneration* 36.

[12] Monroe C. Beardsley, *Aesthetics: Problems in the Philsosophy of Criticism* (New York: Hackett Publishing Co., 1981) 564.

[13] Sally Mitchell, *Victorian Britain: An Encyclopedia* (New York: Garland Publishing Co., 1988) 7.

[14] Lothar Honinghausen, *The Symbolist Tradition in English Literature* (Cambridge: Cambridge University Press, 1988) 112.

[15] William York Tindall, *Forces in Modern British Literature: 1885-1946* (New York: Alfred A. Knopf, 1970) 333.

[16] Jackson, *Eighteen Nineties* 66.

[17] Walter Pater, *The Renaissance: Studies in Art and Poetry* (New York: Johnson Co., 1967) 16-17.

[18] Pater, 5.

[19] Pater, "Conclusion" in *Renaissance* 236.

[20] Pater, 236.

[21] Pater, *Renaissance*, 222.

[22] Pater, *Appreciations* (London: Macmillan & Co., 1871) 104.

[23] Jackson, *Eighteen Nineties* 292.

[24] Pater, "Conclusion" 235.

[25] Pater, *Appreciations* 6.

[26] Pater, 7.

[27] Pater, "Preface" in *Renaissance* 7.

[28] Pater, 7.

[29] Pater, 28

[30] H.E. Gerber, *Edwardians and Late Victorians* (New York: Anchor Books, 1986) 60.

[31] Edgar Allan Poe, "The Poetic Principle" in *The Complete Works*, Vol. 14 (New York: Thomas Y. Crowell, 1902) 274.

[32] John Ruskin, *Selections from the Writings of John Ruskin* (London: George Allen, 1893) 6.

[33] Christopher Ricks, ed., *The Poems of Alfred Tennyson* (Berkeley: University of California Press, 1987) 393.

[34] Rabindranath Tagore, *The Religion of Man* (London: Unwin, 1970) 57.

[35] Arthur Symons, *Dramatis Personae* (Indiana: Robbs-Merrill Co., 1923) 97.

[36] Symons, 94.

[37] Symons 96.

[38] Symons, 54.

[39] Arthur Symons, *Studies in Art and Prose* (London: J.M. Dent, 1904) 284.

[40] Symons, *Dramatis Personae* 97.

[41] Symons, *Studies in Art and Prose* 284-285.

[42] Katherine Lyon Mix, *A Study in Yellow* (Kansas: Kansas University Press, 1960) 1.

[43] Arnold Hauser, *The Social History of Art* (New York: Vintage, 1987) Vol. IV: 187-188.

[44] C.S. Lewis, *Allegory of Love* (New York: Oxford University Press, 1958) 55.

[45] Happold, *Mysticism* 152.

[46] Jackson, *Eighteen Nineties* 132.

[47] Kelley, *Fellowship of the Saints* 57.

[48] Hugh Walker, *The Literature of the Victorian Era* (Cambridge: Cambridge University Press, 1921) 120.

[49] Walter S. Houghton, *The Victorian Frame of Mind 1830-1890* (Massachussettes: Houghton Mifflin Co., 1968) 231.

[50] Houghton, 23.

[51] R.K.R. Thornton, ed., *Poetry of the Nineties* (London: Penguin, 1970) 150.

[52] Thornton, 151.

[53] Thornton, 166.

[54] Thornton, 166.

[55] Thornton, 236.

[56] Thornton, 162.

[57] Thornton, 128.

[58] Pater, "Conclusion" 236.

[59] Vincent O'Sullivan, *Poems* (London: Elkin Mathews, 1896) 60.

[60] Masao Miyoshi, *The Divided Self: A Perspective of Literature of the Victorians* (New York: New York University Press, 1969) 72.

[61] Vincent O'Sullivan, *Aspects of Wilde* (London: Constable & Co., 1936) 212.

[62] F. C. Happold, *Mysticism: A Study and an Antholgy* (London:

[63] Penguin, 1973) 48.

[63] Happold, 49.

[64] Happold, 49.

[65] Joan M. Ferrente, *Woman as Image in Medieval Literature: From the Twelfth Century to Dante* (New York: Columbia University Press, 1975) 5.

[66] Carl Jung, *The Archetypes of the Collective Unconscious* (New Jersey: Princeton University Press, 1968) 212.

[67] Ferrente, *Woman as Image* 67.

[68] Herbert J. C. Grierson, ed., *The Poems of John Donne* (Oxford: Oxford University Press, 1966) 336-337.

[69] Thomas Kelley, ed., *The Fellowsphip of the Saints: An Anthology of Christian Devotional Literature* (New York: Abingdon Press, 1948) 634.

[70] Rollo May, *Man's Search for Himself* (New York: Dell Publishing Co., 1953) 92.

[71] May, 90.

[72] Northorp Frye, *A Study of English Romanticism* (New York: Columbia University Press, 1963) 8.

[73] Frye 33

[74] Richard Summer and Georg Roppen, *Strangers and Pilgrims: An Essay on the Metaphor of Journey* (Norway: Norwegian University Press, 1964) 7.

[75] Frye, *English Romanticism* 46.

[76] Happold, *Mysticism* 47.

[77] Paul Tournier, *The Person Reborn* (London: SCM Heinemnn,

1966) 74.

[78] Arthur Waugh ed., ***Samuel Johnson Lives of the English Poets*** (Oxford: Oxford University Press, 1952) vol. I: 4.

[79] Jaroslav Pelikan ed., ***Twentieth Century Theology in the Making*** (New York: Fontana, 1971) 56.

[80] Thomas à Kempis, ***Of the Imitation of Christ: Four Books*** (Oxford: Oxford University Press, 1940) 16.

[81] A Kempis, ***Of the Imitation of Christ: Four Books*** 19.

[82] Merritt Y. Hughes, ed., ***John Milton: Complete Poems and Prose*** (Indianapolis: The Odessey Press, 1957) Book III, 11. 1-25.

Chapter 11
Poems: The Soul in Heaven's Court

In *The Dark Night of the Soul* John of the Cross presents the tribulations that await the soul in its journey that will take it to the court of heaven where the union with the Divine is expected to take place. In his book John of the Cross, first, outlines the multiple pitfalls that every individual has to overcome in his effort to reach spiritual perfection and then elaborates in detail the function of the two nights of purgation. The first night, says John of the Cross, is associated with the sensual part of the soul, and the second, with the spiritual part. The journey is overwhelmingly filled with temptations such as pride, lust, and the rest of the deadly sins. When the traveler eliminates all the obstacles, then and only then, he is ready to move to the second night. Of course, many years may elapse before the penitent moves from one stage to the next. It should also be noted that no matter how strong the soul is it is always in need of God's help in order to succeed in this very difficult quest. Finally, man should always remember that the journey is indispensable if his soul is to unite with the Divine.[1]

In the same book John of the Cross compares man's journey to the journeys taken by the saints. The journey, he claims, is from the City of Destruction to the Heavenly Jerusalem or from Egypt to the Promised Land. It is also from the dismal swamp of evil to sunlit Mount Carmel; and finally, from the blind and stormy night of sin west of the land of night and darkness to the transcendent morning light of the east. Most importantly, man realizes that the quest in question is inward, and hence not a physical one. Therefore, the quest is defined as a process, a spiritual transformation occurring in time rather than space, and the light toward which man travels is God's brightly-lit court that actually exists in the human heart.[2]

There are three steps that have to be taken in order to attain perfection. The individual feels the urge to take the journey in the first place, a journey he knows will ultimately lead to Divine union. So that the first step involves the reasons that prompt the soul to decide to go forth. Obviously the soul has come to a realization that it cannot go on living in sin. The soul shows determination to suppress any desire it possessed, up to the present moment, for all the worldly things. It is time to deny all the senses. The second step deals with the means the soul chooses to achieve its aim. For this reason the soul has to select a specific road on which to travel. That road is a metaphor for faith. Faith, says John of the Cross, is an emotion, essentially a matter of the heart that cannot be understood by the workings of the mind. The third and final step examines the point toward which the soul will journey, namely God, who remains fully incomprehensible to the sinful soul in this life. These three steps translate into three nights that the soul is required to experience before achieving the Divine union.[3]

Spiritual life is a journey in which man discovers himself in the process of discovering God. John of the Cross points out the fine distinction that exists between the false self that is not in communion with God and the true self that is. Illusion or shadows first overwhelm the true self and then continue to transform it into a false self. Thus the true self is expected to break the shackles of sin and dissolve the masks of illusion. As such, man's obligation is to eliminate the false self because it stands between his true self and God. The urgency to regain the true self becomes the only objective for anyone who decides to attain the union with the Divine. In this world fame and success are the myths of the ego that divert man continuously from his main goal. Yet even in his most sinful moments, in God's eyes, man remains the great pearl for which Christ gave all upon the cross, in order to possess him as His own.[4] This simultaneous presence of light and darkness, of truth and falsity, is one of the paradoxes of spiritual life.[5]

The mystical journey described by John of the Cross appealed to Vincent O'Sullivan thus, he decided to imitate it in his two collections of poetry. O'Sullivan virtually guides the reader from Hell to Heaven through Purgatory by creating a very influential persona who is seen going through multiple trials and tribulations until he reaches the court of heaven.

Poems begins with the painful and unbearable state of Hell from which the persona tries to liberate himself using the traditional means of repentance, prayer, and resistance to sin.[6] The temptations depicted are powerful and at the same time, the persona's will not strong enough. The reader witnesses the sinful persona and wonders whether he will make it to Purgatory, where he would be given a chance to prepare his soul for the final union with the Divine, or whether he will continue to wallow in sin?

In the opening poem *To his Soul* Vincent O'Sullivan deals with the sinful persona urging his soul to go forth on a journey of purification. This is the first poem where the reader encounters the poet creating a persona who in turn projects his soul. The poet creates a make-belief relationship between two friends wherein one of them insists that the other "go forth" to "find some fair pleasaunce." The two friends represent the persona and his soul locked in an internal dialogue. Having realized how sinful he has been, the persona decides to salvage his soul from the earthly garden where "writhing serpents" prevail. His soul is sent off to find a different garden, a pre-fallen garden, where evil and temptation, symbolized in the "serpent," do not exist. Actually it is expected that the soul will find peace and joy in the heavenly garden, these are the same feelings the soul enjoyed before it came to earth. Presently, the soul is depicted drugged a state that results from sinning. The soul has been living in a land where the "moon is red" and where the "star is falling, and a poison light falls thy sweet life to mar." In this same place where the soul has been residing "little toads and gliding lizards thrive / in the damp grass" the idea of hidden evil is fully implied.

At nightfall the feeling of agony intensifies, and the persona seeks to hide since the nagging urge he feels to send his soul forth before daybreak, in the hope of cleansing it, becomes a glaring reality. As a matter of fact, he shows signs of impatience because he is afraid that he might change his mind before his soul sets forth on its quest. He trembles at the thought that his courage to hold onto his decision might weaken. In the poem O'Sullivan refers to the purifying "fire" which will cleanse the tormented soul of "lust and foul desire." In the last stanza the persona's urgency in his attempt to send off his soul before dawn is once more emphasized. Again, he mentions the fear of daybreak with the possibility of going back to his habit of loving and accepting his soul in its ugliness. Moreover, he is afraid that the very act of accepting his sinful soul will weaken his resolve to save it. The sinful soul makes Christ "bereave" as it falls deeper and deeper into sin by continuing to commit "deeds of shame."

This poem introduces the reader to one of the important themes of the collection, the desire of the sinful soul to save itself. By choosing the subjective mode the poet makes the collection look more like a personal drama, a common practice with many poets at that time. Like most Decadents, O'Sullivan takes on the pose of the sinner so as to provoke the complacent Victorian reader to look at the spiritual state of man. This poem, like all the others in this volume, is religious. Many poets, before O'Sullivan, asked similar questions about the opportunities religion could offer, but in this volume the poet lays down his own religious queries and worries. Each poem adds, builds, emphasizes, repeats, and develops what the previous poem presents.

The influence of various metaphysical poets is detected in this volume since O'Sullivan seems to have borrowed from them not only themes but also the methods they used to present these themes. The poet dramatizes his ideas by using dialogue between the persona and his soul. In this way the poet successfully turns his personal abstract experiences into concrete ones. By dramatizing his ideas he chose action rather than dry and ineffective description of situations. No one can overlook the influence of John Donne and George Herbert in the way O'Sullivan created dramatic situations. In addition, he borrowed from Henry Vaughan the religious quest taken in order to purify the soul before its unity with the Divine. Finally, from Richard Crashaw he learned how to use mystical experiences common to man and Saint and transform them into verse. But he also borrowed from Crashaw the idea that Saints become successful intermediaries in man's attempt to unite with the Divine.

This collection celebrates spiritual love by using, at first, physical love with all its sensuousness, gradually the poet undermines the physical by choosing a purer diction. O'Sullivan decided to use this technique in order to convey his conviction that the spirit can redeem itself only through the acceptance of the flesh and not by its rejection. The question he poses and tries to answer is what can man do to defeat the flesh and rise above its boundaries to Heaven? The flesh is symbolized by the numerous references to the grave throughout O'Sullivan's poetry. Hence, once in the grave, the flesh will fade away and the soul will be set free to roam back to the arms of the Divine, of course, with the help of the Holy Virgin who has been interceding all along.

According to Catholicism, sin is an act against the law of God. He who sins mortally deliberately turns away from God, seeks life in whatever is opposed to Him, rejects God, and enthrones his enemy. After sinning, man is utterly blind and lives in darkness. He cannot see the light of Heaven shine any more. It goes without saying that if grace is not granted to him he cannot come out of darkness. To overcome sin man has to go through a complete conversion, a transformation of being; only then, can he hope for a reunion with God to take place. Sin, theologians believe, separates man from God. To obtain union with God man has to receive His grace that will help him through mortification and self-abnegation, as well as self-renunciation. It is not enough for man to believe in Christ, more is demanded of him. He has to act in order to rid himself of his sins, of course, always with God's help. Theologians stress that without the grace of God and its aid is certain that man will fall and whoever falls from grace and lives in sin falls further into sin. Actual grace is required in order that he may be upheld and strengthened in the hour of conflict. Consequently, man, is given a choice to either return to God or continue to live under the domination of the devil. But one thing is certain, he cannot return to God without His grace and before purifying his soul.

O'Sullivan uses the metaphor of courtship and marriage extensively in this volume. The heart is the Bridegroom's chamber, the temple ordained for His marriage to the soul, but He must stand outside and knock. "For the heart has calcified in the ways of the world, and the spouse dwells entranced by its false lights." The chamber must be prepared for its guest. It must be purged with the fires of remorse and love, and cleansed by tears of repentance which are "the distillation of the *incendium amoris* thus ignited." Only then may He enter and bestow the kiss and the ring intended for no one but His bride.[7] Deep in the heart of man the Bridegroom wishes for his nuptials with His spouse. "What lowliness and loftiness" exclaims Saint Bernard, "to be at once the tent of Kedar and the shrine of God, an earthly dwelling and a heavenly palace, a clay hut and a royal hall, a mortal body and a temple wherein dwells the Light, scorned by the proud and yet the Bride of Christ."[8]

Salvation is liberation from man's sinful selfhood. Man is continuously attacked both from within and without by a variety of destructive forces. Liberation from these forces is a prerequisite in attaining salvation. To achieve salvation man does not have to die. All he needs to do is turn to Christ and open his heart to His love and grace.[9] Man's life on earth, among other things, is supposed to be a preparation for the life to come, a life to be lived in the presence of God. But congenital sinner that he is, his deliverance is dependent on receiving grace through Jesus Christ. To establish the right relationship between himself and God man has to atone.

O'Sullivan continues to develop the idea of the sinful soul that makes the persona's life miserable in the next poem. In *According to Thy Mercy* the persona is depicted suffering a guilty conscience, but, most of all, regret for the kind of life he has led so far. During the night when he is lying in bed he "sweats and shakes from fear" and his "aching soul is tossed." He remembers how he has spent his life seeking for "worthless praise, vanity, pride" and all other sins among people, while at the same time he forgot the existence of God. Suddenly, the persona is reminded of Christ's mission on earth and especially His sacrifice to save mankind, including his sinful soul. And even though he has forgotten Christ, the latter has kept watching over him with "loving zeal" hoping that the moment will arrive when he admits his sins for the first time. That time has come and having accepted his sins the persona begins to feel remorse and shame, and asks for God's pity. Gradually, he also realizes that he was a fool to doubt God's power and "blind to join the army of the lost." At this moment of illumination he wishes to die because that is the only way he can devote himself to serving God in Heaven till the end of time. Only death can help him refrain from sinning again. When he asks God to "take now my life, my breath, / If thou wilt save because I sorrow so! / To serve till death," the reader notices the despair into which the persona has fallen. In this poem, O'Sullivan defines the particular sin the persona has committed as that of "angry lust" for which he is asking God's forgiveness and pity. The poet depicts man's soul engaged in battle with the powerful enemies of evil that makes the personal drama of sin and repentance more intense and vivid. After all, man has to consciously strive for a union with the Divine as the only way to keep spiritually alive. Thus the union with the Divine should be man's main goal in life and he should strive to make it the essence of his very being.

In *Knight of Dreams* O'Sullivan chooses the medieval romance for the context of his poem as well as medieval images and ideas to convey his experience. He also draws on the Arthurian legends when he refers to the knight who is preoccupied daily with discovering methods in an effort to save a human soul. The knight is in church in front of the altar waiting patiently to hear God's "soft word" before he sets off on his quest. While expecting his command from the King he is seen

> ... riding forth upon a day in the summer,
> When sunshine dances gaily through the wind,
> He hath a hail for every gentle comer,
> And blessing for all folk of honest mind.

The poet goes on to say that the knight "changes in joust and tourney" as he tries to do "a deed for God on each day's journey." In the last stanza, he encounters "a body in its starkness" that is the body of a man possessed by the devil. A group of monks have surrounded the body and are trying very hard to save it from the clutches of evil, but to no avail. The image expresses the view that the persona's soul is controlled by the devil, as long as it lives in sin. The sinful persona is fully convinced that it has to turn to the "knight of dreams" for his salvation. As for the knight, he has no choice but to engage in battle with the devil to save the persona's soul. The poet describes the knight approaching the body as well as the steps he takes to exorcise the evil spirit. After an arduous battle the knight saves the possessed soul. He is satisfied to have won one more lost soul for His Father, the King. The poet captures effectively the feeling of awareness the persona attains of his sinful condition as well as his desire to make amends. Moreover, the persona is portrayed trying to find the means that would most definitely help him get out of his miserable situation. Throughout the collection the poet refers to prayer, repentance, and doing penance as the first steps toward salvation. All the means of salvation are evaluated as to their effectiveness and the question that arises in the reader's mind is whether the persona will finally find the appropriate means to save his soul?

This volume of poems takes on the structure of a medieval play as the poet dramatizes the whole process of salvation where Saints and the Virgin Mary appear to mediate on behalf of the persona/sinner. Into this structure O'Sullivan enmeshes features of the medieval romance where knights are seen engaging in battles in an effort to save the distressed souls from the clutches of the devil. The poet stresses the virtue of these knights as well as their faith in God. These two qualities help and encourage the knights to succeed in their undertaking. However, this volume is also about meditative poetry where all human faculties are utilized to apprehend the presence of God. O'Sullivan uses striking and often sensuous imagery to record religious issues as well as the technique of dramatization wherein the soul is witnessed in intense meditative experiences. Thus these poems are accounts of memorable moments of self-knowledge and union with some transcendent reality, in this case, the Divine. In fact, the reader observes the poet first projecting his soul upon an imaginary stage, and then scrutinizing it in order to understand it, of course, always with the help of the Divine presence. In the process he hopes to succeed in either understanding the essence of his soul, or else fail to do so and ultimately be led to endless despair. In his effort to explain the complexities and contradictions of life the poet adds an intellectual quality to his poetry. Yet no one can overlook the powerful emotions that permeate his poetry. Emotions such as physical love, religious devotion, desire for Divine union, and fear of death, are the most significant. His poetry can also be easily labeled metaphysical because, even though he blends secular and religious elements, he succeeds in going beyond them. After all, his major theme is his concern for man's soul and his salvation. Most of his poems have the form of a debate held between the persona and his soul, sometimes between the soul and God, and in some other instances between the persona and the Holy Virgin. Notwithstanding the simplicity of the diction, and the emotions conveyed by each are very intense.

O'Sullivan's persona expresses a deep love for the Holy Virgin as his prayers prove. Thus his prayers reflect the effort the persona exerts in his attempt to triumph over his false self, an indispensable step if he wants to unite with the Divine. As Quiost says:

> ... the first act of communication between man and God took place through Mary, and it was in Mary that the act was accomplished. In her, as the embodiment of the highest human perfection,

which had been prepared from the beginning of the world, all men and all of the earth were brought into the presence of God; and God was brought into the presence of man and of the world.[10]

Saint Bonaventure said that the Virgin is the intercessor, the mediator through whom God reaches man and man reaches God. Moreover, she is man's defense against sin. And since man reaches God only through woman then the Holy Virgin provides the way for all of mankind.

>I call upon the Eternal Father
>through his Son, our Lord Jesus Christ,
>that through the intercession of the most Holy Virgin Mary,
>the Mother of the same God and Lord Jesus Christ,
>and through the intercession of Blessed Francis,
>our leader and father,
>he may enlighten our eyes of our soul
>to guide our feet
>in the way of that peace
>which surpasses all understanding.[11]

As has already been pointed out, in the previous chapter, women have both a symbolic and an active function in the salvation of man. "At every stage of the upward journey they guide by love and prayer, by criticism and example." As "reflections of God, as symbols of virtue and love, they draw out the good that is in man" and "as loving and compassionate beings, they bring the straying man back to the road of redemption with their criticism, and help expiate his sins with their prayers." Therefore assumption that all women, not just the Holy Virgin, can be intermediaries between God and man by showing love, moving man with their inner beauty, and touching God with their prayers cannot be ignored.[12]

The *Norman Cradle Song* is a different type of poem. It is the first of many lullabies in this collection, in which the poet starts by depicting a mother holding her baby in her arm and trying to lull it to sleep. The image the poet wants to suggest is that of the Blessed Mary holding Christ. Metaphorically, the sinful persona visualizes his soul held in the arms of the Virgin Mary and as such protected. When O'Sullivan shifts to expose the persona's thoughts the idea that man's soul would be safe only if God held it in His arms becomes wishful thinking. This happens to be the first poem in which O'Sullivan uses the supernatural element since the song deals with a "sea-elf" that wanders during the night in the churchyard. The sea-elf comes from the sea and visits the town it loves best. When the elf comes to town it walks toward the churchyard in order to visit the beloved's grave. At the first sign of dawn the elf vanishes. The elf and its beloved form the metaphor O'Sullivan uses to depict the separation between the persona/lover and his soul/beloved that presently is dead and lying in the grave. This metaphor is intended to suggest the death and loss of man's soul. The fact that the poet is using the supernatural element means that the very situation he is trying to describe is abstract at the moment. Without question the idea of ever achieving a union with the lost soul remains, at least for the time being, as far-fetched and intangible as the appearance of the elf that comes and goes. In this poem, O'Sullivan deals with the sea and the mother for the first time. From the Jungian point of view, the poet deals with death and the grave symbolically. Both the sea and the mother refer to the womb and the grave respectively. Both are the places to which the persona wishes to withdraw because he believes that there he will find his lost soul.[13] The elf comes from the sea to visit its beloved's grave and disappears again into the sea. Indirectly, the persona is expressing a desire to die and experience the grave in hope of finding his own lost soul which he believes exists in another world that is, in the abyss for some time now. Obviously, the poet is referring here to two inter-related prevalent ideas: that of the grave being the passage that leads to the lost soul, and that of escape from the physical world of pain.

  In the following poem, *Lament*, O'Sullivan repeats the concept of death, in that the death of the beloved reflects the death of the persona's soul. In this way the poem is linked with the previous one. But there is also a slight difference between the two poems in that the former poem dealt with supernatural beings while this one deals directly with the persona and brings the reader back to the human level. He begins his poem by describing his beloved before her death.

> Deep eyes that gathered laughter from the skies,
> Thy cheeks of red-white roses bathed in dew,
> The hands like cool quaint-fashioned ivories,
> The spun-gold hair with sunbeams dallying through,
> And soft grace and dainty fragrance caught in the sweet South.

But all these beauties have become extinct now that she is dead. At the present moment all he sees is "this gray-white thing." The persona/lover refuses to accept the death of the soul/beloved so he goes on to revive the memory of the beloved as she used to be before her death. He actually clings to the way she used to be in the past avoiding, in this way, the pain of having to face the present. By withdrawing to the memories of the past he experiences all the old feelings he had for her. This poem reflects a common practice for a poet who tried to escape the world of the nineties by creating a fantasy world where beauty reigned supreme. At the same time, the persona says that "he yearns to sleep with [her] in slumber sweet; / Rest we together 'neath this drenched rose-bush." The separation from his beloved is unbearable and so he expresses the wish to unite with her in death. But after a little while he changes his mind about uniting with her at the present moment; instead, he tries to imagine a happy life with her in the future. He says: "And we shall dream away the sultry hours, / Or sleep-flushed hark to small birds carolling." He takes hold of her "thin hand" and wishes that this time, at least, he would vanish into these "passionless hill-flowers" until the end of time.

The first and last stanzas describe a state of joy and

peace thus emphasizing the fact that life with his beloved/soul can make the difference. The second and third stanzas, that form the mid-section of the poem, deal with the separation from his beloved/soul as well as the loneliness that he feels as a result of this separation. These feelings are quite different and contrast with the feelings exposed in the other two stanzas. Finally, the poet chooses to have silence permeate the poem as the lover grieves the loss of his beloved. He hopes that the day will come when he will transcend the painful present moment and achieve a state of eternal joy with his beloved. One should not forget that O'Sullivan is describing the state of the persona's soul as it was in the past that is, when it was innocent. As long as the persona's soul was innocent it shone with the radiance of God's light and beauty. But one cannot but be inquisitive about the present state of the persona's soul. Not only is it dead but it is also awful to look at actually, it is an object to be shunned. Naturally, the persona wishes to point out that by remembering the past he emphasizes the fact that he yearns for the time when his soul was pure. He also mentions death and lying in the grave as a means of achieving a union with his lost soul and possibly, redemption. The idea of dying and entering the grave to find the beloved/soul is another theme that links this poem with the previous one. Only that in the first the elf willingly returns to the sea that suggests death, while here the lover procrastinates and decides to join the beloved, not immediately, but some time in the future.

 Absence of the beloved as the result of death reflects the separation of the soul from the body, and the metaphysical separation of the human soul from the Divine. The image of the separated lovers that appears often in this volume explains the incompleteness man feels when he loses his soul, as well as the loss he experiences when he falls from God's grace. Consequently, the desire to find the beloved and unite with her is nothing more than a desire to achieve completion. A necessary state before any attempts to reunite with the Divine are made. The anguish man suffers is twofold because not only does he feel torn from his soul, he also feels distant from God

If he succeeds in finding his soul, then, and only then, will he defeat pain and transcend to achieve the desired mystical union with the Divine.

In his sermons John Donne expresses the incarnate dynamism of humanity with the metaphor of married love: "As farre as man is immortall, he is a married man still, still in possession of a soule, and a body too." Death, he tells us "is the Divorce of body and soule; Resurrection is the Reunion."[14] The metaphor for the love of husband and wife serves for the union of body and soul. Donne wrote about death and resurrection in figurative language as the separation and reunion of a loving couple. Moreover, death brings the disintegration of the body: "Then the dust returns to the earth as it was and the spirit returns to God who gave it" (*Ecclesiates* 12:7). O'Sullivan uses the same ideas and metaphors Donne used before him. On analyzing his poems it is difficult to ignore the influence of many metaphysical poets on his work

In *By the Sea-Wall* O'Sullivan describes death as a fearful shape, it is likened to a horrible witch that is invisible yet capable of haunting man. Still this witch wanders freely around us and inflicts fear in our hearts. In the poem the persona sends his "cream-white bird with the scarlet mouth," to his beloved in order to keep her company, to sing to her, but also warn her of the "death witch" which is freely wandering looking for the opportunity "to snap away her life." The witch is seen weaving a shroud, which she plans to use to trap the persona's beloved. The beloved lives on an island making it very difficult for the lover to go to her at any moment, hence his decision to send her the bird instead. The island stresses the separation between the two. Once more, the poet links the sea with death since both are present simultaneously. Of course, the fact that the beloved lives on an island far away from her lover is a repetition of the same idea conveying the separation of the persona from his soul. Furthermore, the beloved is trapped since she lives in isolation on the island surrounded by the sea and, at the same time, under the watch of death. This makes a union between the lover and his beloved almost impossible. As the poem concludes the death witch approaches the beloved, and puts her arm around her "musk-rose body." This very act suggests that the witch, finally, fulfilled her deceptive plan since she walks away with the beloved/soul. O'Sullivan conveys effectively both the witch's victory as well as the lover's defeat. The persona suddenly realizes that in order to unite with his soul he has to go through the kingdom of death, in other words, he has to plunge into the sea. What is new in this poem is the persona's decision to enter the grave immediately overcoming in this manner any procrastination he has had as the previous poem has shown. The persona expresses a degree of certitude that death is, after all, the only possible means that can lead to the consequent union with his soul as well as its salvation. In this light, the persona transforms the witch into the nymph of death that will guide his soul through the dark passage of the grave. She is the woman who is sought and not shunned. Certainly, the persona has changed his mind about the woman since he starts believing that the female figure has something significant to offer him. As a matter of fact any suspicions he has had of her disappear.

The Peace of God is another poem about the sinful soul that has lost the grace of God. It is different from the poems that preceded and have dealt with the same theme because, for the first time, the persona admits his sins. Henry Vaughan's poem *Regeneration* comes to mind, wherein the poet says: "In the one late paines,/ The other smoake, and pleasures weigh'd / But prov'd the heavier gaines."[15] Similarly, O'Sullivan says that the persona by choosing pleasures in life was led to ignore the "Mystic Queen." "Strange scarlet things of sin and flame. / A housing in the home of sin; / From Thee to these I ached to win, / And hid thy glory in my shame." Now he is ashamed of his past behavior and turns desperately to the Virgin Mary to pray for help. He wants her to light up a "lamp" so he can "gain Thy presence soon." His sins have darkened his vision and hence there can be no return to the path of righteousness. To find his way back he needs light, in other words, he needs the grace of God. Suddenly he realizes that his wish has been granted because he believes he can detect some figures even though the mist still lingers. It looks as though the darkness that has blurred his vision for so long is finally beginning to lift. He sees, at last, the figure of Christ on the cross and his attention is drawn to His haggard face. He also notices the "crown of thorns." It is significant that he sees the crucified Christ because that reminds him of pain and death, but also of redemption. As his vision clears, he begins to realize the importance of Christ's mission. At the same time, he decides to atone for his sins, and pray to the Virgin Mary to intervene on his behalf. Somehow the decision to change his life brings along a feeling of peace even though he fears that that might prove to be temporary.

In *A Cold Night* the poet once more deals with the theme of death. He describes a morbid atmosphere by evoking the feeling that everything around him is frozen. The persona's attention is drawn to a dead woman who is lying alone. The persona cannot seem to ignore the woman's "stiff gray face" that "is furrowed with scars." Then the poet moves on to describe another woman who is present as "gaunt" and who, he finds out has come from the "Frigid Zone." This woman is no other than the death witch of the *Sea Wall*. She is mysterious and resides in the 'Frigid Zone." Death in O'Sullivan takes always the form of a woman since, in this way, he can associate with her the concept of the temptress. Thus it becomes easy to depict situations where man is trapped by the beauty of a woman, or by her wiles. O'Sullivan borrowed the idea of the woman/temptress from the Romantics. In this poem death is not only personified, it is also seen in action as opposed to her recent victim that is passively lying cold. It is clear that the persona is both aroused by the dead woman and frightened by the "gaunt" lady. O'Sullivan expresses the dilemma many of his contemporaries faced when considering death as the only means of salvation and, therefore, very much desired. But at the same time they doubted whether death might prove an adequate solution. O'Sullivan describes the natural surroundings in this poem as cold and lifeless. The descriptions are intended to suggest death as the "sparrow" has frozen, and a "starved dog" cannot find any food so he "gnaws at an icy bone." The cold wintry night is an appropriate choice since it evokes successfully the theme of death. On the whole, death is the most powerful and prevalent feature of the picture he is painting.

A Christian considers death as the most significant event in man's life. From the religious point of view, it is a part of man's progress, not the end, toward God's embrace. Thus for the Christian dying goes further than simply the withering away of his individual world. It is actually the only means to be initiated to immortality. Theologians argue that when the belief in immortality is knocked away, the dying man is left to cling to the material world as long as he can, and then slide into oblivion. It is no wonder then that he struggles, often with very little dignity, to hold, however tenuously, to life. That is why he considers death an archenemy, the final inescapable disaster. Finally, man's life becomes a feverish attempt to avoid not only death itself but also the thought of it.

> Lo! I tell you a mystery, we shall not all sleep, but we shall all be changed, in a moment, in the twinkling of an eye, at the last trumpet. For the trumpet will sound, and the dead will be raised imperishable, and we shall be changed. For this perishable nature must put on the imperishable, and this mortal nature must put on immortality ... then shall come to pass the saying that is written: Death is swallowed up in the victory (*I Corinthians* 15. 51-54).

In the *Rose Witchery* O'Sullivan continues to use the contradictory states of life and death and succeeds in making them look almost identical. For the Decadents living during the *fin-de siècle* was not any different from being dead, and being dead was a desired state, as has already been mentioned. The poet begins by describing a woman lying on the grass by the stream. For the first time, the poet selects a pastoral scene for the background of his poem. In this landscape the beauty of the living woman is intended to imply innocence and peace. In the second stanza the woman is not alive any more, but dead and lying in her grave. Obviously the persona is comparing the two states of his soul, first, when it was pure and full of life, and now that it is sinful and dead. His soul experienced two contradictory states: first, when it existed in a paradisiacal state and lived in joy because it was close to the Divine, and presently as it experiences torment because it is in Hell. Again the soul is in the grave, and here the persona comes to sprinkle roses on the grave. The rose is chosen by the poet because it links the two states, for the persona is reminded that he used to give his beloved roses when she was alive, and now that she is dead he again brings her roses. As for the woman she is at the center of the two states. The lover is seen trying to keep the memory of his beloved alive with the help of the roses. The reader witnesses the persona trying to cling to the image of his beloved when she was alive in order to suppress the present image of her as a dead woman. The rose, which is used symbolically, is chosen by the poet to convey this unconscious behavior. As the present recedes into the background the past comes vividly to the foreground, and even prevails for a little while. The joyful times the persona has lived are referred to by the felicitous singing which continues to echo in nature and which, reminds him of the past. On the contrary, sorrow presently prevails and the only music heard is that of wailing and lamenting. Clearly, nature is depicted as sympathetic to the persona as the wind echoes first the joy of the past and then the sorrow he feels at present.

In *The Lady* O'Sullivan describes the lady especially the "glamour of her laugh" and "her red mouth, and her teeth" as the persona holds her. But this feeling of joy is marred by the thought that very soon she will die and lie under a tombstone with an epitaph upon it. Throughout the poem the poet shifts between life and death. The white hands that she nurses with such care, and decorates with "bracelets and old rings" are being prepared for the "slimy" worms. The obsession with the lady's death makes the persona foreshadow the moment when he will be standing by "her bier." The fear of her death interferes with his present feelings. The fear is so deep that it prevents him from enjoying the present moment. Unlike the poem that preceded here O'Sullivan does not move between the past and the present instead, he chose to move between the present and the future. The present moment is annihilated by the shadow of the morbid future. The future holds deep sorrow that blurs the present moment of joy. Here the poet introduces the theme of transience for the first time. The knowledge of the transience of beauty, youth and joy becomes an obsession that he cannot rid himself of. He realizes the inevitability of death and the unavoidable natural process of decay, and is seized with deep fear. In this poem the poet expresses his apprehension of death as opposed to the passionate desire to experience death as already mentioned. The persona goes as far as resisting the idea of death as a part of the natural process that leads man's soul from earth to Heaven; from temporal life to immortality. Furthermore, this is the first poem in which the persona is holding the beloved in his arms. He is not willing to let her go because he is alarmed of losing her forever. This suggests that the persona/sinner has succeeded in regaining, after a very long time, his soul. Yet he cannot overcome his fear of losing it again. It is this panic of separation that explains his attempt to shun death.

Pirate-Wife's Song is the second lullaby of the volume in which O'Sullivan once more describes the mother lulling her baby to sleep. The subject of her song is about the actions of her husband who happens to be a pirate. She relates how the pirates seek out merchants and their ships as they travel "the ocean with bags of gold, / And fine goods win by their greed and sin." At the same time the merchants "scuttle and flee" when they detect the pirate ships that pursue them. The mother continues her song wherein she tries to explain to her baby the actions of the pirates. She says that they do what they do because they have to feed their babies. So violence, or even death, that might be brought down on the sailors, is justified since the cause is good. Again the poet links the mother with the sea, and simultaneously with the idea of death since the pirates ran the risk of dying by drowning or sentenced to death when caught.

White Dreaming also deals with the sea but unlike the previous poem the persona looks at the sea, and deals with death instead of sleep. In the vast sea, he says, there are numberless "ghosts" that walk and wail a clear reference to lost souls. The poet describes an incident where the persona struggles to save someone from drowning. He happens to be on a ship that is caught up in a tempest, and he is trying to save his friend from "the haughty dancing foam." Suddenly he awakes and realizes that it was only a nightmare. The realization that his body has to drown in the deep of the sea is hard to accept. In his dream he recalls that he tried desperately to prevent his body from sinking to the bottom of the sea that is, he tried to withstand death. This means that he is not yet ready to let go of the physical, of the body, or life on earth. This poem reverses the determination the poet has shown in *By the Sea-Wall*. He actually finds it hard to choose between his desire to let go of life and his wish to cling to the status quo. Since O'Sullivan uses the sea as the equivalent of death then it is clear that the persona is referring to death, and is trying hard to avoid it. Death scares him; it is actually a nightmare, especially when he recollects his dream. Unquestionably, the incident symbolizes the loss of his soul to sin. It is this realization that frightens him, and of course, he is relieved when he becomes aware that it was only a bad dream.

The *Children's Hymn on the Coast of Brittany* is another prayer to the Holy Virgin and Christ, as it concludes with the word "Amen." O'Sullivan refers to Christ's childhood when his mother used to lead him by the hand so he would not get lost. "Like us, He could not find his way, / Although He was Our Lord, the King: / And so we beg we may not stray, / Nor do a sad or foolish thing." So the persona asks the Holy Virgin to lead him too, now that he is certain that he is lost. But he does not wish to be led only for a little while; instead, he wants to be protected and led throughout his life, since it is so difficult to resist temptations alone. This minute detail in Christ's life fills him with courage because, if Christ had to be led, then what about him who as a common layman has the tendency to easily stray. In this poem the persona expresses the wish to be placed in the protection of the Holy Mother. He also conceives that prayer is the distilled awareness of man's whole life before God, it is meant to lead man to a radical transformation of consciousness in which all of his life on earth becomes nothing but a symbol. Prayer is an elevation of the soul to God, the soul's affectionate quest for God or a conversation between God and the soul, and it is used for expiation and thanks, through it man's union with God becomes possible.

The theme of loss is taken up in the following poem *Ariadne*. Here O'Sullivan uses the pagan myth of Ariadne who, with the help of a thread, led Theseus out of the labyrinth, for his own purposes. In addition to the myth introduced the persona dreams of a beautiful woman whom he compares to a shining star that lights up the dark night. "One great star that lamps the night / Breathes reproach upon my strife, / Its calm gleaming sets me dreaming / All the evenings of my life. / Ariadne." The woman the persona sees this time resembles a Saint and not a witch. He imagines she is soaring upward to Heaven making it difficult for him to either approach her or follow her. The theme of the poem is about the woman guiding the sinner, whether this is Ariadne, the Holy Virgin, or a Saint. It is evident that the persona needs a guide to lead him out of the abyss and away from temptation and sin. The poem ends with a feeling of uncertainty of what will happen to him since there is no sign that the persona has found the woman who will help him. Will he be able to detect her in the dark night since he is "blind with tears," or will he be able to see the bright star that can guide him to "the Silver Courts of Heaven" as it has guided the three Magicians to Christ's manger in Bethlehem? The question is left unanswered.

Papillons du Pavé is the first poem of the collection in

which O'Sullivan refers to a social issue of the nineties. The poem describes a butterfly "braving the city's heat," that is, male sexuality and social attitude. The persona identifies with this woman who feels an outcast. He describes her colorful appearance since she is wearing a lot of make up but does not fail to notice that underneath there is so much misery. He intentionally chooses the red color in order to imply passion. He identifies with her because he believes that she, like him, shares a blighted life. She is fed up with people's attitude toward her, but all she can do is "fling her sudden weary laugh" at them as she walks down the street. O'Sullivan uses a prevalent social problem in order to express a religious theme. The sinful soul of the persona is identified with the harlot. Similarly, the persona disregards people's comments about his ways as he continues to walk down the streets of life tasting the forbidden fruit. Finally, the idea that the "butterfly" is trapped because of her lifestyle resembles very much the way the persona feels. In general the reference is mainly to the feelings the poet of the nineties experienced in his own milieu. "A butterfly, a poet in vain, / Whose life is weeping in his mind, / And all the dreaming of his brain / Is blighted by the dusty wind."

The sinful soul needs to pray and that is what the persona does in the next poem, *Unto the Throne*. God is described as "saddened" because of his sins, but also "gladdened" since he begins to join the legion in rendering his puny praises to God. The poet describes the persona

>... chaunting with the legions thunderous
>To the God obscure and wonderous
>All the carols that his false mouth used
>>before to sing to crime.
>Of the passions in his breast
>Which outflamed and murdered rest,
>Lo! the chars are pieced together and
>By Thee are made sublime.

For the first time the persona thinks of praying and is

seen doing so. Thomas à Kempis believed that man, and especially the sinner, had to offer a specific prayer to Christ when asking Him for help and grace. The prayer reads as follows:

> O merciful Jesus, enlighten Thou me with a clear shining inward light, and remove away all darkness from the habitation of my heart. Repress Thou my many wandering thoughts, and break in pieces those temptations, which violently assault me. Fight Thou strongly for me, and vanquish the evil beast, I mean the alluring desires of the flesh; and so peace may be obtained by Thy power, and that Thine abundant praise may resound in Thy court, that is, in a pure conscience.[16]

And as the sinner continues praying for God's grace he hopes to be transformed. In this light à Kempis says:

> Pour forth Thy grace from above, imbue my heart with heavenly dew, supply fresh streams of devotion, to water the face of the earth, that it may bring forth fruit good and excellent. Join Thou me to Thyself with an inseparable band of love; for Thou even alone dost satisfy him that loveth thee, and without Thee all things are vain and frivolous.[17]

The Knight reappears in order to serve God after having fulfilled his mission since the sinful soul has decided to follow God's path and become one of His knights. The persona refers to his "foul soul" that has been for long in the devil's possession. He had even forgotten that Christ had sacrificed Himself for his sake. It seems that the Holy Ghost breathes into him, an act that inspires him because suddenly he feels the need to confess and repent. The dark path is lighted and the sinner/persona decides to be led by an inner impulse. At last, the persona has found the path that will lead him to the King who, as the reader discovers later, intends to dub him as one of

His knights. The sinner/persona feels like singing with "the quiring host," an urge he never felt before.

In *Two Voices* the persona finds himself in the middle of a group of friars but unlike the previous poem he does not join with them in prayer. Somehow he finds it difficult to pray and that, because he is reminded of how heavily his sins weigh on him. The poem is about that inner voice urging him to join in prayer the friars and the voice of his conscience reminding him of his sinful present state. He sits under a tree, and falls into a trance as the friars' prayers fill the air and are carried over to his ears. In his trance he sees the friars approach the altar praising God, the Father, and Christ. "There floats the praise of Holy God; / Oh Jesus Christ Who our earth trod / The God Who lives, the God who died." Suddenly, he becomes aware that he is not with the friars and wonders why. But he recollects what is keeping him away. It is because his "heart is sick" and his "brain is fire." As the poem nears its conclusion the persona realizes that joining the friars in prayer is a far-fetched idea. During his trance, his vision is beclouded and, as O'Sullivan says, a "mist" shrouds everything, and "a ghastly scarlet sin" swallows everything in the darkness of the night. The sinner is in the dark labyrinth again, lost and alone, afraid and desperate at the thought that he might never get out any time soon.

In *Dirge* O'Sullivan once more deals with the death of the beloved who is about to be laid in the earth. She is unable to hear the sound of the sea, wind, bird, or the "groaning of the trees." Nor can she hear "the skylark's trill," "the shouts of girls and boys, / The plashing brook" or "the creaking mill." Yet she can hear the sad voice of the persona singing a dirge and sadly repeats the refrain "to sleep, to sleep" intensifying the mood he wants to evoke. It is a mood of total passivity and despair. It is noteworthy that in this poem the persona depicts the peace that can be attained only in the grave. Furthermore, one witnesses the desire of the persona to join the beloved in her new abode. That is the second time, after *By the Sea-Wall*, that the persona considers taking drastic action and letting his soul enter the grave. Obviously, he has come to accept the concept of death and the idea that the grave is of utmost significance if he wants to save his soul.

In *Brain Fever* O'Sullivan uses the theme of sickness, a theme that prevailed in the literature of the nineties. He creates a situation where a man who represents the persona is lying in his bed raving as a result of high fever. As he raves he brings to the surface what lies deep down in his unconscious. At the beginning, the sick man is conscious of his surroundings because he looks out the window and notices "the pale leaves through the window blow / And roses wither in the heat." But once he loses touch with his environment he relives the time when he was out at sea on a ship. Like S.T. Coleridge's Ancient Mariner, he sees "A strange ship! for her sails are shrouds, / Her hull the four planks of the dead." He believes he can discern a passenger, but it turns out to be no other than "a derided wreck / Of life, this weary broken man." Obviously, the wrecked passenger symbolizes his wrecked soul that has become estranged from him, a sight he cannot help shuddering now that he looks at it. "Horror! this hateful face I know! / It is Myself I hail and greet." The persona feels ashamed of the changes that have affected his soul. He feels pain especially when he realizes that his sickly condition is spiritual rather than physical. The poet repeats the third and fourth lines to convey the sense of decay that prevails, and to remind the reader that the vision the persona has had of the past state of his soul is only momentary. The poet chooses to put his persona/sinner in bed so as to stress the fact that the persona is passively accepting his present condition. There is no sign that he is either willing to change his condition or that he has the strength to effect any changes. And as he drifts off to sleep he shuts out his fears and pain, and prolongs a condition which is static since it does not lead anywhere.

O'Sullivan continues to compare the present state of the sinner's soul to what it was like in the past *In Window Lights*. Here the persona imagines God's hands sending him grace as in the old times, that is, before he became a sinner. How different things were in the past when he was "almost free from the stains of crime" and when he bowed before God, the Father, to pray. It is as though his guardian angel protected him from "the devil's snares" and taught him how to pray. He even recalls that the sun had formed a crown that would be set on his head when he dies. But now things have changed so drastically, and all because he was so weak and could not resist temptation, thus he cannot expect to "win [a] crown, [or] gain [any] palm." How disheartening everything seems now that he "can win no crown, can gain no palm." The poet makes it clear that there is no hope whatsoever for the persona's soul to be saved. The only way his tormented soul can find peace is undoubtedly, through death. Yet, the question that haunts the persona is if death can offer him the peace he is seeking or will it yield another kind of suffering. Most importantly, he wants to find if death will lead to Hell and consequently more pain. Clearly, the poet is alluding to the fires of eternal Hell that intimidate the persona and make him procrastinate to accept death as the only solution for his tormented soul, although he does not answer the question he poses since he does not know the answer yet.

On the contrary, à Kempis believed that there was hope for man when he says: "Blessed are they who are glad to have time to spare for God, and shake off all worldly impediments. Consider these things, O my soul, and shut up the door of thy sensual desires, that thou mayest hear what the Lord thy God shall speak in thee." And again "Thus saith thy Beloved, I am thy salvation, thy Peace, and thy Life: keep thyself with Me, and thou shalt find peace." And the advice that has to be followed is to "Let go all transitory things, and seek those that be everlasting. What are all temporal things but seducing snares?" After all, what can "all Creatures avail thee, if thou are forsaken by the Creator? Bid farewell therefore to all things else, and labour to please thy Creator, and to be faithful unto Him, that so thou mayest be able to attain unto true blessedness."[18] O'Sullivan puts his persona in a position which requires that he makes a decision as to whether he is to give up this world or the world of Heaven.

Sea Sounds is the third lullaby in the volume where the mother reappears with the child in her arms. But it is also a prayer since the mother does not intend to lull her baby to sleep only, but also to ask God to protect it from possible nightmares in the present as well as hardships in the future. "Oh, my child, when you are older, / And at night you set the sail, / May no harsh wind strike you cold." Once more, the reader is told that the child's father is a sailor. The center of her prayer shifts to him as she prays to Jesus to keep him "from the cruel creeping / Mist and frost-rain keep him free." She predicts that her child will become a sailor some day just like his father. She continues to pray for her husband to return to her and her son "back to you and me/ Bring him safely back to me." The repetition of the last line in each stanza adds to the musical effect of the lullaby and helps the baby fall asleep.

Following the technique of the dialogue used earlier in order to enable the persona to talk to his soul, O'Sullivan writes *Caitiff's Rhyme*. In this poem the persona gives a final message to a friend that happens to stand for his soul: "One last message ere I rest / I must send." He first conveys his feelings and ideas about God and heaven, and then compares life on earth to a form of bondage. The persona tries to find the courage to ask forgiveness from his friend, who represents his soul in this case, for having wronged him. He says that he wants to "borrow one hot sigh, / To curse the man who brought you sorrow." The persona/sinner admits that he has followed the wrong path, and the fact that he wants to curse himself for destroying his soul is a sign that he is experiencing another moment of awareness. The question is whether the persona/sinner will do something to change his hopeless condition or will he continue to lament his fate. The action the persona decides to take is outlined in the following poems.

Fairy's Music is the poem in which we see O'Sullivan's persona escape from the earthly to the supernatural world. He needs time to think and meditate and come to the right decision, but obviously he cannot do that on earth because it is so full of temptations. This is the second time the poet uses supernatural beings, which as he says, can bring joy to nature with their song. The fairies come at midnight and spread laughter and kisses and sit on a "rose or a lily," and when they leave their breath is full of flowers. Stanzas one, three, and six add to the musical effect of the poem and are intended by the poet to amplify the melody and harmony that prevails in the supernatural world while simultaneously juxtaposing the disharmony that exists on earth. This other world, the fairy world, becomes a very alluring one. The fairies see a "cosset" all alone its mother has turned away for a moment to take care of another one of her young ones. They approach it, promise to watch over it, and assure it that no harm will ever come to it. The fairies then call out to Eleuthera who vanishes because she fears a lizard. She continues to remain lost since the fairies look for her in the waters as well as in the woods. Their search does not yield any fruit. As the night wanes and the last star in the sky is noticeable, the fairies realize that it is time to go before the sun rises or the priest appears for the morning prayer, or the milkmaid goes off to the dairy. The persona's dream bursts like a bubble and with it the temporary escape it offered. Certainly the persona was freed from his worries for a brief while. In the poem the persona is looking for another world, a more joyful one, maybe it is only a fantasy world which he can create by his imagination, but unquestionably it is totally different from the real one in which he lives. At the end of the poem he finds himself all alone and wallowing in despair as at the beginning. Obviously, the supernatural world is not a lasting one, or one to which he can cling to for long since it disappears as fast as dew drops.

It is known that in folklore and primitive religions fairies symbolize the supra- normal powers of the human soul, at least in the forms in which they appear in esoteric worlds. They are personifications of stages in the development of the spiritual life of the soul. The fairy world, therefore, is presented as the equivalent of the world of Heaven and the fairies are no other than happy souls that have already been saved. The fact that the persona refers to Heaven as a fairy world suggests that he cannot discern it clearly yet, for it is still abstract and far-fetched, and vanishes from the mind's eye as fast as the fairy world.

In his fourth lullaby *Old Mother's Lull-to-Sleep* O'Sullivan tries to keep the joyful atmosphere of the previous poem vivid as the mother's song to her little girl Aline shows. Through the lullaby the mother expresses a wish for her baby. She hopes her little girl will dream that she is "a wee fairy queen." She hopes that the little girl will not have to undergo the rough times she has been through. Instead, she reassures her that next day will be beautiful and happy when she goes out to the shore to play with "coloured shells" and "tiny laughing waves." She even looks forward to hearing her daughter's dream next morning. She is keen to find out about the meeting with the fairies and what the "elves" told her when they were sitting alone under "the white moon." The persona gives the little girl the opportunity to experience a situation that he desires, but cannot have, because he has lost his innocence. The child is chaste, and therefore, able to talk with the elves. Only the pure can transcend to another level of existence. Obviously even her mother cannot come close to the fairies because she, too, has lost her innocence. So she has to wait till next morning to find out from her daughter what the fairies have told her. The fairy world is depicted as pure and ideal. Can a grown-up experience this world, or will he have to settle for the child's account of it? This poem stresses the painful realization stated in the previous poem. The peace and harmony of the fairy world seem to be out of man's reach. Instead, man seems doomed to taste bitterness and feel disappointment. The only hope of joy left for him is the child's account, no wonder then he is seen clinging passionately to it. As has already been said the child can see the happy world of Heaven because it is innocent and pure at heart. O'Sullivan borrows this idea from William Wordsworth who dealt with it successfully in his poem *Intimations of Immortality: An Ode,*

Wordwsorth described the child as the only means man has to experience Heaven as a grown-up, and the child's account the only reminder of "the visionary gleam" that has vanished, irretrievably.[19]

A Triumph is placed intentionally by O'Sullivan almost in the middle of the collection. It is the poem that summons a turning point in the life of the persona. The sinful soul has finally overcome its false self and has triumphed over temptation as the title suggests. But the question that still persists is will this victory help the persona climb out of the abyss in which he has been lying for so long. If he dies, will he be able to transcend to the ideal world of Heaven which he has, up to this point, envisioned as supernatural and, so far, attainable only by the chaste child? The poet alludes to the fact that the persona/sinner is either raving or dreaming and that results in confusion and lack of clarity. This is the first time that the persona's soul appears in front of him. It is personified since it appears in the shape of a woman with whom he starts immediately to converse. He can see "the sad strange languor of [her] eyes." These eyes remind him of the "sweet days that ne'er have died." These were the days when his soul was strong because it was pure. He goes on to refer to the coming of Christ to earth and the fact that Christ took pity on him and decided "to save this mean man." He begins to see "the splendent graces flowing, flowing / From the grace within His eyes." At last, God's grace is being sent to him. Finally, the persona acquires the strength to turn his life around. The love Christ has shown him gives him the power to turn a new leaf. He is reminded of Christ's words: "I am the way, the Truth, and the Life" (*John* 14.1). Thomas à Kempis referred to the same idea when he said that man should follow Christ because "without the way there is no going; without the truth, there is no knowing; without the life, there is no living." And again à Kempis states that without Christ no one can find the Truth because as Christ said only "if thou remain in my way, thou shalt know the truth, and the truth shall make thee free, and thou shalt lay hold on eternal life."[20] Hence the persona decides to withdraw to a hermit's cell to pray and do penance. But he does not want anyone to know the location of his cell, because he is afraid that the devil will seek him out and try to tempt him all over again. Hiding in a grave would prove to be the right thing to do maybe then the devil would also ignore his existence. However he is seized with terror as it dawns on him that the devil may be able to read his thoughts. So he turns to Christ for help and protection.

> Before thy coming I fall down,
> High God in whom all worlds meet
> Let me draw near and feel Thy feet,
> And bite the dust cast from Thy gown.

He implores Christ to stand by him in his attempt to defeat the devil. Even though he has resolved to leave all earthly pleasures behind and seek the peace, the loneliness, and the security of the cell, he is still afraid of the possibility of falling back on his old self. *A Triumph* marks the turning point in the sinner's drama. From here on the point of illumination and the final return to the pre-fallen state is imminent. *A Triumph* represents the climax, the moment the soul has to deal with the forces of the flesh pulling it downward and the forces of the spirit pulling it upward. This is a tormenting conflict that O'Sullivan casts in the form of the medieval psychomachia. The reader witnesses the soul of the persona finally triumphing, and the poems that follow, express a feeling of relief experienced after the longed for freedom from the prison cell of the body has been achieved. Evidently, the persona has, at last, decided to place his body in the grave so as to free his soul and send it off to Purgatory. His major wish has, finally, become a reality. He feels better as he is virtually moving out of the abyss of Hell and into Purgatory. Of course, the persona is aware that he has a long way to go still before he attains the innocence and purity his soul once possessed, as well as the joy of Heaven which follows the ultimate union with the Divine.

Hermit's Harrow continues the theme O'Sullivan

presented in *A Triumph*. After retiring to an isolated cell and leading a hermit's life the time has come to test his resolve and strength in dealing with temptation. A beautiful woman appears right in front of him in his cell. Her hands are described as "twin lilies," a symbol of purity assumed as a disguise by the maiden with the intention of tempting the hermit. Outside a tempest is raging and the "ships on a desolate shore" are anchored waiting for the storm to subside. The storm symbolizes the tempest that arises in the hermit's soul the moment he sees the beautiful lady. The psychomachia that occurred in the previous poem is repeated here as the soul feels both the upward and downward pull once again. The appearance of the temptress is nothing more than a test that the persona's soul has to overcome. She wants to lure his soul away and as such effect a rift between him and God. Seized with fear and full with passion he hears the woman exclaiming "Jesus, our Savior, have mercy on me." These words are supposed to mislead the hermit. Immediately he experiences a conflict between his sinful old ways that prompt him to return to them and his present life of restraint. He is convinced that the woman who has entered his cell is pure so he decides to kneel before her. But suddenly, he feels that her physical beauty is extremely luring and feels weakened. Instantly, he turns to the Holy Virgin for help. This is the most crucial moment in the persona's quest and praying to the Holy Virgin proves a good idea. Since the Virgin Mary is the intermediary between man and God, and since through her the persona hopes to come closer to the Supreme Being as well as obtain the grace needed for his salvation praying to her is the only thing that is reasonable to do at this moment. As is already known, the Holy Virgin represents the point where human and Divine meet in the flesh. Furthermore, it is also known that the Virgin Mary regained God's love for man. It is through her love and humility that God took flesh in His Son. The persona offers the woman a bowl of "the end of all craving," "the balm of hot rancour and raving," and "life's sweetness and saving." Not suspecting him in the least, she takes up the bowl and drinks the "poison." She collapses and the hermit in a paroxysm of joy begins to dance and sing for having defeated temptation presented to him in the guise of purity and chastity. He feels relief for the time being as well as stronger for succeeding. He has defeated his "blacker soul" and has come, a little closer to Jesus. The death of his false self gives birth to the true self. At last, he has found the way to salvation through his resolve and faith to defeat evil. At the same time, calm, follows the storm out at sea. For the first time, the persona is experiencing calm and peace but the question is whether this state will last, or will he have to face more trials and tribulations before he attains lasting peace. O'Sullivan attempts to answer this question in the next poem.

In *Hermit's Harrow* O'Sullivan projects evil by personifying it when he describes evil waiting around the corner to attack the hermit. Using personification does not mean that O'Sullivan believed that evil existed outside of man. He simply used the method because he wanted to concretize the persona's spiritual experience. As has already been said he did conceive evil to be a part of the persona's self. And since both good and evil exist deep in man's psyche man has to turn inward to find the Image of God as well as the image of the beast, the devil. Moreover, man has to remember that the image of God is defaced by sin but restored through the sacrifice of Christ. Man has not simply fallen he has achieved redemption from the Fall as well. Thus it is man's responsibility, with the omnipresent help of grace, to clear and renew the Image of God, until it becomes a true similitude. But because this renewal can never be wholly accomplished in this life man usually ends his life with a cry for help, a prayer for some momentary glimpse of perfection, and a hope that regeneration will be completed after death. Finally, man realizes that in order to comprehend Good he has to acquire full knowledge of evil first.

In *Night Voyaging* O'Sullivan returns to the theme of the journey. The penitent sinner is depicted venturing out of his cell, hence out of the abyss, out of Hell. Symbolically, he comes out from the deep darkness after defeating his false self.

Having reached Purgatory it is time to travel on and do more penance. So the persona is seen taking a walk with a child on the wharf where many vessels are anchored. As he strolls he reads the names painted on the vessels. There is "God's Gift" and "Heart-ease" and "Dreamland" before which he, and the child, come to a halt. The child he is leading by the hand is symbolic of his own soul that is being led in its new path by Christ, to whom he has so fervently prayed. He enters the ship and sails off into the night, an action symbolic of the transition he has already gone through. The ship slides over the waves and "pleasantly rocks on the sad sea's breast," leaving behind "grim doubt and regret." He sails on for a while before he stops at a churchyard, where he discovers that those who lie there "sail on and on to the golden west" and "never return!" He realizes that no one should cry for them for the "tired must rest." It is evident by reading this poem that the boat trip is analogous to the mythological trip taken down to the kingdom of death where Pluto welcomed the souls. The persona's readiness to die is shown and the trip is, at this time, pleasant and offers what he has desired for so long, the peace of the grave. A peace he could not experience before because his soul was rotting in sin. By repeating the refrain he stresses the fact that he is tired and that the desired rest is not far off. Time has come to sail "to the golden west!" Now he is sure that the life of the grave is essential if he is to break free from the shackles of his physical condition. After all, salvation comes definitely only through the grave and the death of the body. The body, as such, is held responsible for all the pain the persona has undergone. Only when his soul is liberated from his body will it be redeemed from earthly torment and allowed to enter Heaven to enjoy the peace, joy, and harmony of the pre-fallen world.

Having discovered and chosen the spiritual way *The Cathedral* becomes the center of attraction for the persona. It is an old cathedral that attracts the attention of the traveler/persona who goes through the "narrow streets" of the French old city. The traveler feels "anxiety and pain" until his eyes fall on the old church which looks "fresh and young" even though it has "time's harsh stains" on it. The church stands "sublimely" above the town and defies time. It is a church over whose towers "monstrous evils rolled" and it came out unscathed. Now it stands upright and "solitary, grand. / A wondrous triumph magnificently old." It is a structure that will go on standing proudly for it has achieved its place in Eternity. Like George Herbert, in his collection **The Temple**, O'Sullivan identifies the persona's soul with the old cathedral that has overcome many battles with evil, and finally, stood victorious.[20] From this moment on, the persona believes he has found the path to salvation and is assured that the worse is over. The "monstrous evils rolled" over like the sins of the flesh, and the only thing that has survived is the Cathedral, which the poet used to represent the soul, that Divine gift to man. The soul that regains its shine, freshness, and purity has defeated the passions that made it look old and ugly. Now that his soul is liberated from its bonds it has the strength to overthrow the "monstrous evils" at any time they dare challenge it. At last, he feels a "wondrous triumph!"

The journey toward redemption continues in the next poem *In the Road*. Now that the penitent persona has come out of the abyss he has to continue his journey until he reaches his final destination, which in his case, is no other than Heaven. Until now his journey has been torturous and full of tribulations, but it seems that the journey will continue, without respite, to be full of hardships for some time yet. He is seen travelling through the cold dark night of the grave toward the warmth of the green fields like Henry Vaughan's repentant sinner who is led

> Full East, a faire, fresh field could spy
> Some call'd it Jacob's Bed;
> A Virgin-soile, which no Rude feet ere trod,
> Where (since he stept there), only go
> Prophets, and friends of God.[21]

Like Christ he has to harrow hell before he is ready to ascend to Heaven. As he lies down to repose, momentarily he hears the voice of Christ addressing him as a "poor sad son" and reminding him of the efforts he has exerted in order "to gain thee with My wounds and tears." This reminder could not have come at a more opportune time. The traveler is instantly filled with the courage and the capacity to travel the dark road that lies ahead. Christ offers him "a lantern filled with soothing oil" to lighten his road. The traveler/persona is elated for his journey is different now since Christ has asked him "to make thine abode with Me," and if he accepts then all "his red crimes" He "will assoil." The persona/sinner has evidently come a long way. His penance and prayers have purified him to a large extent and is presently told by Christ that he will be cleansed of his "red crimes" as well. At this moment he feels such spiritual strength that his "pride is overthrown" and as a result, his soul becomes a great deal lighter. Without asking any questions he puts himself in the hands of Christ. One witnesses the influence of another Metaphysical poet on O'Sullivan's poetry when obediently, like the raving feverish priest of George Herbert's *The Collar*, the persona answers "My Lord, My God, I am Thine Own."[22] He finds the new abode satisfactory and resolves to cling to it forever. He recalls that he had yearned for long for this peace of mind. How sweet is the feeling of tranquility after an arduous and torturous trip. How light is his soul, and how easily it can push onward now. For the first time his soul is enjoying freedom after the last sin, that of pride was shed. How long, he wonders, will he have to travel before he finds the gates of Heaven.

In *Wheat and Clover* O'Sullivan uses again the technique of the dialogue between the persona/lover and the soul/beloved. But this time it is different because the lovers are together and are seen wandering holding hands, carefree and happy while the birds sing in the trees "a wild song of delight. / In the splendour and drowse of the soft moon." The setting is quite different from what it used to be when darkness and cold prevailed and the lovers were separated by the harshness of death. Here the lovers never stop talking to each other, even though they are not paying close attention to every word that is being said. They continue to walk "happily hand in hand / [their] souls serene and [their] hearts at rest." In the last two stanzas the reader discovers that the beloved has died a long time ago and that the lover is old and "bent and gray." He admits he has died along with her, and along with everything else around them. The song of the birds changes instantaneously. The lover begins to cry and his "blinding tears" disable him from seeing his lost beloved coming toward him. But there is no need for tears since his false self has died and his true self -- his soul/beloved-- has been resurrected. Interestingly, enough the persona refers to the past so as to suggest that the salvation of his soul took many years to achieve. As he looks at the wheat and clover he sees his soul/beloved rising from the plants. The process of resurrection occurs in a pure and natural surrounding. What O'Sullivan implies is that the soul of the penitent has been set free to travel to Heaven. Evidently that death had to precede this revival. The old relationship between body and soul is abandoned for the new one between the wheat and the clover. The rebirth of the persona/sinner is finally realized. The significance of using the clover in this poem is immense. The clover symbolizes the Trinity because of its tripartite form. The union of the wheat and the clover foreshadows the union that will occur with the threefold God when the persona's soul is fully purified.

  Unquestionably, O'Sullivan believed that a sinner could be saved only if he turned to Jesus, opened his heart, and asked Him to enter. "No doubt, the advent of God in a man's body and in human life, that is the physical or historical Incarnation, is already complete."[23] But the mystical Incarnation of Jesus' coming to each man, into man's life, and the life of the world, has been perfectly accomplished by the love of Christ, yet has still to be realized in time by means of man's free response. "I am the vine, you are the branches," said Jesus, "make your home in me, as I make mine in you" (*John* 15.4-5). "But just as not all of the vine's branches reach maturity, so too not all men are one with Christ; not all men make their home in Him."[23]

According to Saint Bonaventure, "Christ is the way and the door; / Christ is the ladder and the vehicle."[24]

The lovers having reached the state of purity that is, the persona/lover and his soul/beloved, continue to travel to *Lake Glamour*, the land of the fairies. In the moonlit night the lover bids his beloved goodnight. The fairies are getting ready for their night ramble and the "water maid" "clings to the oar" as she glides down the calm stream. This is the land that he could not enter when his soul was tainted by sin. This is the same land he had to hear about from the child's account the next morning. Now that he is there he is ecstatic to be journeying in it. But the final stage of purification is yet to take place. After its accomplishment he will be hopeful of the union with the Divine that is, the marriage with Christ and that, at this point, does not seem far away.

Before the union with the Divine occurs he has to pray a little while longer. So *In the Hymn to St. Dominick* O'Sullivan shows his persona praying to Saint Dominick whom he describes as a special Saint who traveled to Spain to preach "mankind not to err." The Saint "brought'st His peace to every door. / And soothed'st the hind's sore back." At the same time the penitent is reminded of Christ's sacrifice and of his ultimate act of love. The persona realizes that he has to pray to the Virgin Mary for every bead "plants one of virtue's seeds," and "all errors that the devil planned" will fall off into the void. The reader is told that Saint Dominick's life, like that of Christ, ended one "bleak wintry night," and like Christ, Saint Dominick is now in "Heaven's Court [where] thou takest thy rest / With Christ our Lord thou dost consort / Thy head upon His breast." In this poem O'Sullivan describes the union of the Saint with Christ and indirectly foreshadows the union of the persona with Christ. The persona has to pray to the Saint to intercede on his behalf. O'Sullivan's persona/sinner is not any different from Richard Crashaw's sinner who prays to Saint Teresa to cleanse him. "Against this Brest at once break in / And take away from me self and sin." And Crashaw goes on to say:

> By the full kingdome of that final kisse
> That seiz'd thy parting Soul, and seal'd thee His;
> By all the heav'ns thou hast in Him
> (Fair sister of the Seraphim)
> By all of Him we have in THEE;
> Leave nothing of my SELF in me.[25]

From now on all the repentant persona has to do is get ready for the final union. The fire of Christ's love will purify him thoroughly so that the final stage of his long journey will shortly take place. The union is the persona's ultimate goal and the most meaningful reward. It is only after the union with Christ that he can become one of His knights and reside in the King's court.

Woman's Song is the fifth lullaby in which the reader sees the child in his mother's loving arms being lulled to sleep. It seems right to mention that there are slight differences between this lullaby and the previous ones. Only the quiet harmonious song of "the wet green bird" is heard as it fuses with the mother's lullaby. For the first time the mother does not refer to the sea, and the world outside is peaceful. This change in the mother's lullaby signals the fact that the persona's soul is now lying in the arms of the Holy Mother like Baby Christ. Once more this lullaby is also a prayer since the mother prays to God to protect her child from the evil fairies and to give it only happy dreams. She prays to "our dear Lord's Mother" to protect her child from the "old Man's wiling" who "go gliding / From her chiding," and who is watching for an opportunity to harm him. The reference is to the devil that is seen hovering trying to find the appropriate moment to seize man's soul.

The following poems show a different mood and tone since the persona's soul has transcended to a happier state of existence. The poet describes and refers to situations that take place in the spring as opposed to the cold nights of the winter through which he has already lived. In *Garden Fantasy* the persona's attention is drawn by a butterfly as it "hover[s] flitting there and here," and "dances without a sign of fear" bearing a "message from [his] dear." The persona/lover, the reader is told is not presently alone for he is with his beloved/soul contemplating the moment when his soul will unite with the Divine. By the end of the poem the "pranked messenger" alights on the persona's fingers. Doubtless the persona has learned the language of the butterfly because he is capable of decoding the message sent to him. Obviously Christ has transmitted a message to the persona. The choice of the butterfly is significant for two reasons: first because it is symbolic of the soul, and second, because it is attracted to light and as such represents the persona's soul attracted by the Divine light. Furthermore, the cleansing process continues and the soul will become lighter and eventually capable of flying toward the Divine like the butterfly.

Catholics explain the mystical way by dividing it into three stages: the way of purgation, the way of contemplation, and the way of union. The way of purgation has two major objectives. First, a complete renunciation of sensual things, and the death of the self so that the Divine may be born in man's soul and the union with Him be attained. And second, a continuous cleansing of the perceptions, an incessant scouring of the windows of the soul, so that the light of a new reality may stream in and completely illuminate and transform the soul. "The kingdom of Heaven is within you; hold fast to thy center and all things shall be thine."[26] As a matter of fact, the mystical way is said to resemble a slippery slope from which man can slide back to the sinful and unholy life. When the mystic decides to go on the quest he has to strip away all encumbrances so that the light of Heaven may be able to enter his soul. Gradually when he begins to be illumined he is led to the state of contemplation where his soul witnesses the Divine image. A glimpse of the Divine in all things is the first actual change the mystic experiences. After the soul is absorbed by Divine love it is set free to enter the domain of God. Naturally the penitent finds himself closer to God and is blinded and dazzled by His light. Time has come for the soul to undergo the last phase of his experience that of merging with God in an everlasting union.

In *On a Day* the persona asks the little "blithe" bird to sing a song along with him in praise of his beloved. The bird is seen hopping from one bough to the next chirruping happily. The choice of the bird suggests the transformation of the lover. The bird's song, the reader is told, breaks the morbidity of the cold wintry landscape. The persona is seen bearing fresh flowers he has picked himself, to his beloved. The "offerings of flowers," a combination of violets, roses, and lilies are fresh and fragrant. Momentarily, he is seized with the desire to immortalize his beloved by carving her name on the barks of the trees. In his opinion, this act will not maim the trees; instead, he believes each tree will be proud to bear her name through time. And in the days to come when she will not be there and he will wander amongst the trees alone, he will be able to kiss the inscription of her name and revive her memory. It is inevitable that everything will wither and fade away since "above our heads harsh winter-time doth hover." Once again O'Sullivan deals with the theme of transience, but with a variation, since the persona has learned to accept the passage of time -- something he could not bring himself to do earlier. There is a drastic change in his attitude because he has come to know that without death there can be no life, in exactly the same way as there can be no spring without winter. Time, the destroyer of physical beauty, is responsible for bringing about spiritual beauty and immortality. Going through the grave in order to achieve the immortality of Heaven becomes, not only a natural process, but also the only acceptable way.

In *Sancta Dei Genetrix* O'Sullivan depicts the birth of Christ. The Virgin Mary is seen holding Him in her arms as she traverses the market place. This is the first poem in which the poet refers specifically to the identity of the mother and her child. The purification of the persona's soul has eventually cleared his vision and that is why the poet uses the particular instead of the general. In other words, he is able to depict exactly the identity of the mother as well as her child. He wonders if the "weird children" in the marketplace noticed her. Naturally the innocent children would be able to see her while the adults will fail to do so. He even asks if the children have noticed "the sunshine in her face." The poet goes on to describe the pain and sorrow the Holy Virgin underwent when her beloved Son was taken away to fulfill His Father's mission. He wonders if these children who "toddled by her side" succeeded in relieving her pain for a while, or if they "made her smile."

It is evident that the persona is not only relieved of the pain and the tension, he is also seen resting from his tiresome journey. Of course, this does not mean that he has to stay in this garden forever. In the garden he can feel the "breezes straying from the Court of God," breezes which inspire him and purify him before he sets out again. He still has some way to go before the final union occurs. In *Spring* he speaks of dreaming of the "soundless, soothing hours" he has experienced as opposed to the nightmares he has had in the past. But he feels it is time to return to the active way. As the flowers come to life and bloom in the spring, and the spring showers revive nature from its deep winter inertia; he, too, feels the urge to make use of his innate energy to achieve the desired union with the Divine. The choice of spring is meaningful, since it represents the renewal of nature as well as the parallel rejuvenation of the persona's soul.

Saint John of the Cross distinguishes between the sensual and spiritual soul, and then goes on to describe the active and passive modes which the soul has to choose from. In **The Ascent of Mount Carmel** he exposes the active mode of purgation through which the sensual and spiritual souls traverse while in **The Dark Night of the Soul** he outlines the passive mode of purgation. In his poetry O'Sullivan uses both forms of purgation and dramatizes them in the process of depicting the journey of the persona.

Man can find no rest, final peace, or joy for his soul as long as he sees the borders of light only from a distance and as long as he believes he is an alien, a wayfarer, or a stranger. He has to try to reach the land that lies beyond the stars. Man, before the fall, was a citizen of heavenly Jerusalem but after sinning he became a pilgrim. Once he learns this truth and accepts it he can direct his endeavors to returning to the heavenly city. Thomas à Kempis says, "thou hast not here an abiding city; and where so ever thou be, thou art a stranger and pilgrim; neither shalt thou ever have rest unless thou be most inwardly united unto Christ."[27] Similarly, in their book ***Psychotheology: The Discovery of Sacredness in Humanity*** E. Martin Stern and Bert Marino say:

> To obtain a human vision in Zen is to lose consciousness in order to attain a pure consciousness or formless self. In Christian and Jewish doctrine it consists in perfecting the Covenant between God and man, sacrilizing time and human relationships. East and West meet at the point where moral choice means accepting a psychological paradox which acquires that a man must lose in order to find, become weak in order to be strong, be poor in order to become rich. Both demand the moral courage to seek light from darkness, clarity out of confusion, to leap from one state to a higher one.[28]

Hymn of the Norman Sailors depicts the sailors' nostalgia for their beloved and their homeland as they spend day after day at sea. They know that their sons are praying for their safe return even though they cannot hear their prayer. But on the ship there is one sailor who has mortally sinned and the Virgin Mary expresses her sorrow for him by "wring[ing]" her "gentle hands." Suddenly the ship gets caught up in a storm and the sailors begin to pray to the Virgin Mary for help. The Virgin responds to their prayers and, as the poet says, the sailors can hear her speak to them in the dark night. She assures them that she will remain by their side to "guide" them and "to help lead" them to safety. The persona identifies with the sailors in their distress and fear as he joins them in prayer.

He asks the Holy Mother to have pity on all "that are drowned, / Whose corpses along the tide toss." Using images from sailing, O'Sullivan describes the sinful man as someone who is at the point of drowning. His abandoned body is expected to wash off the shore if the Holy Virgin does not feel sorry for him and saves him. The poet argues that the sinners are lost souls that resemble the drowned men. Only repentance and prayer can help them. Furthermore, from the religious point of view, the waters of the sea are expected to wash off any guilt the sinners have. Certainly the process of purification that will help repentant sinners enter Purgatory, and later give them a chance to pass through the gates of Heaven. After a short respite in *Spring* the persona decides to continue his quest primarily because he feels the need to help others. Now that he has managed to enter Purgatory and is one of God's saved souls, he feels he has to try and win a lost soul for his King. The poem ends with the persona turning to Christ to ask for pity on behalf of sinners. "Through the pains of our Lord on the Cross, / Have pity upon the poor folk that are drowned, / Whose corpses along the tide toss." According to M.V. Kamath a storm functions in the same way as fire; in other words, it purges the soul. "The sudden storm is fierce, for the complacent soul needed a sharp blow to awaken it to the actuality of its own wretchedness and to set it on its way."[29]

  The persona continues his journey until he comes to a stop before the *Statue of St. Vincent de Paul* in Amiens. He recounts how Saint Vincent was deeply loved by children. The children played with him because he was "as simple as a child." His life was "stainless and undefiled." Even though he walked in foul streets he succeeded in keeping his purity "and a sore defeat / Didst deal black Sin which weakling men beguiled." The persona believes that the Saint can intervene to win him the grace of the Savior "because thou art so meek." In his opinion, Saint Vincent can teach sinners to cry and repent for their sins as well as win them back "from direful loss."

  In the last two poems the poet ceases referring to the life and actions of the persona instead, he refers to individuals that the persona meets. This shift signifies that the persona has come to the realization that by imitating the ways of Saints he, too, can help sinners. His determination to help others shows that the persona has not forgotten what Christ and the Virgin Mary have done for him. Helping others also proves that he is capable of showing love for his fellowmen, a quality he has acquired by trying to imitate the life of Jesus. Moreover, he has learned to forgive sinners and not condemn them. This altruism shows how far the persona/sinner has come, and how deeply he has changed. Theologians have pointed out that man can be really free only when he learns to love others without reservation. They also argue that selfishness imprisons man and makes him feel a slave while, on the contrary, love has the potential to set him free.

Breton Lullaby is the fifth lullaby in this collection, O'Sullivan again depicts a mother lulling her baby to sleep but also praying for its wellbeing. She believes his dreams will be sweet because all the Saints and angels pray with her to this effect. Not knowing when the child will dream she tries to imagine the content of the dreams he will have during the night. It could be that he will launch a boat in "tiny waves" or visit a dell where "laughing fairies and nixies dwell." These dreams are so different when compared to her real world, which is depicted as gray, and a place where "the sun seldom shines and the storms are dread." As a matter of fact, by imagining the content of her baby's dreams, she, too, gets an opportunity to escape from her miserable world and live a few joyful moments in this dreamland. She then begins to pray to the Virgin Mary asking for protection and guidance for her child. Finally, she hopes her child will keep its gentle soul "white" and so the light of God will reside in its heart forever.

> Keep then, my darling, thy gentle soul white
> Pure as it is in thy slumber tonight.
> And thy face shall be fair with
>   The flash of God's light.

By repeating the last line in each stanza the poet

emphasizes the child's innate innocence. When the child was still in Heaven "the angels awake thee" every morning. The poet firmly believes that man has to struggle to keep his childhood innocence no matter the cost. As a matter of fact, man begins to slip into the abyss when he loses his innocence and allows sin to prevail in his soul. On the contrary, keeping the child alive in one's heart guarantees closeness to Christ and hence a shield from temptation and sin and, of course, protection from the abyss.

Hymn to our Lady of Peace is the third prayer in this volume in which the persona asks the Holy Virgin to get from Jesus the peace He left for mankind as "benison." It is the persona's belief that this world cannot offer man any peace because it is full of wile. As for "holy peace [it] will only dwell/ In hearts afire with grace." He then moves on to ask for wisdom which will help him distinguish between good and evil. He adds that he is ready to love those who are equal to him, to respect those who have risen above him in society, and who "with worldly honour [were] decked," and finally, to treat fairly the few who are beneath him. The last remark should not be taken as a reference to the social background of the persona; on the contrary, the remark is intended to be interpreted symbolically since it implies that very few have sinned as seriously as he did and fallen as low as he has. But he wants to repent for all of his sins because this is the only way he can win "the peace of God." And he knows that he has to repent real soon otherwise it will be too late. Once more, the reader becomes aware that the persona moves in this poem to the foreground and captures his interest. Unlike the previous poem, mankind ceases to be of any concern for the persona as he begins to focus on himself again. But the thought of breaking away from the obsession of his ego and being of use to others continues to persist. So he begins to pray for all "good folk" but also for the "poor sinners" hoping that they, too, will be helped by the Virgin Mary to "feel one blissful day" and the peace of Heaven, even if that will be a one time experience, and for a brief while. He concludes by assuring the reader that the sweet

"Lady" the "Queen of Peace" will safeguard mankind from "evil blight" every "day and night."

In *The Angelus* O'Sullivan repeats the same religious ideas he has already presented in the previous poems yet with variation. The difference lies in the way he deals with the same ideas and the kind of confidence he shows in dealing with these ideas. He uses a tone, he has developed, which is calm, loving, and forgiving of others. Undoubtedly, the conversion in attitude is the result of the multiple transformations he has undergone as a result of identifying with his persona. As the persona repents and finds the way to save his soul the poet, too, achieves a measure of peace. It should be remembered that the creation of the persona was intended to objectify the poet's personal drama. In this poem one can sense love in every look the persona gives the "good folk." The poet describes the inhabitants of a small town who stop what they are doing and hurry to the church to perform their duty to God and the Holy Virgin as soon as they hear the church bell ringing. The curate pauses "at the corner of the street" and sees "Lucille standeth still / With her lover in the wheat." There is an allusion to the Annunciation and the Angel Gabriel announcing to the Virgin Mary the news that she was chosen by God to give birth to the Savior of mankind. The persona's attention is also drawn by a mother praying fervently and asking Jesus to give her child "rest," because Jesus is every child's friend. And then there are the damsels who come with "faltering feet/Linger[ing] by the wayside cross" greeting "Our Lord" and asking for "truth from final loss." But there is also Margot who writes slowly "with her finger on the ground" the following words:

> Behold the handmaid of the Lord
> Be it done as His own Word,
> Thus spake white maid Marie,
> Queen of all the Angel host,
> I pray gramercy.

Even when the children hear the angelus they stop playing and start praying. And at last, there is mother

Hortense setting violet flowers on her son's grave. The persona notices that she is weeping and his heart goes out to her. After describing everyone around him, the persona turns to himself and asks God to "pour forth into our hearts Thy grace, / That we may run a goodly race." Furthermore, he deems it wise to pray for the light of the Lord in order to see clearly in this world.

Widow's Croon is the sixth and last lullaby of the volume. It is different from all the other lullabies because the mother is not singing, instead, she is lamenting. She is obliged to break the sad news of her husband's death to her child. So she blends the lullaby with the elegy as she describes the rough sea and the small "vessel" which was no more than "a speck" tossing helplessly "through the gusts of the gale and the flows of rain." This detail suggests the defeat of the body as the soul leaves behind the material world to rise above. The vessel is a metaphor for the body and its sinking implies the annihilation of the body. The soul is represented by the child that is in the mother's arms and by implication in the Holy Virgin's protection. It seems certain that nothing can interfere from now on to obstruct the soul from achieving its desired union with the Divine. The mother shifts her attention to the pain her child feels and she starts to soothe its pain by saying that everyone who drowns will rise to "walk in the trail of the storm." She hastens to assure her child that it will never be alone because she, along with its guardian angel, will always be by its side. She concludes by praising "the power of God on the deep" and ascertains that all will rise when Christ and the Holy Virgin return to earth. O'Sullivan repeats the last two lines in each stanza so as to emphasize the power of God on all those who have decided to die, in other words, accepted to drown, and believed that death can lead them to the desired Divine union. The sea is symbolic of life in exactly the same way as the grave that gives life to everyone who dares enter it. It resembles the mother's womb from which all life springs. Last but not least, the purifying value of water as well as the allusion to the sacrament of Baptism should not be ignored.

The poet guarantees that whoever is courageous enough to plunge into the deep sea, or decides to let his false self die automatically will redeem his soul and true self. "The writings of the Fathers speak of the waters of Baptism as both a womb and a tomb. The one being baptized goes down into water as Christ went down into the earth in death. The coming out of the water is Christ rising in glory, victorious over death."[30]

The End of Years foreshadows the end of the collection as the poet depicts the persona lying on his deathbed. Now as a sick man he knows that he will not see the flowers that "will laugh and kiss the wind" or the "blossoms open one by one." This is the moment "when he learns / The secret of his baffled days" as he "listless on his pillow turns, / And slowly shifts his waning gaze." He refers to a child who after vigorous play seeks his bed for rest. But unlike the child the exhausted old man, says the poet, wishes to rest, not for a little while, but forever. He realizes that time passed by very quickly. It seems only yesterday when he was born and yet today he must die because the end has come. He wonders "Whether he slaved or took his ease, / Beleaguered Truth, betrayed his friend," but no matter his actions he has "his weary head in [the] earth" and is about to sleep in "peace." O'Sullivan stresses the brevity of life in order to point out that man has to try and save his soul as long as there is still time. "This is the end," says the persona, a state he has to accept like everyone else. One night "he must wake and stand in an enormous plain / Amongst the dead, who writhe and shake. / To see their buried lives again." His stay in this plain, however, would be for a short time, if his life was good and fruitful, he will see it "re-edified." The persona begins to pray and as he does so exclaims in anguish "pity those poor eyes of ours, / Poor eyes that would, but could not see." This poem describes the panic and fear the persona feels for all who ignore the righteous path until it is too late. Man should not wait until the last minute to defeat his physicality and begin his journey toward salvation.

O'Sullivan repeats the same theme in *Nights of Dreaming* where he describes a bedridden man. As a result of sickness and of not knowing whether he will die, he drifts in and out of sleep. At the foot of his bed he discerns a woman "with the sorrow around her mouth, and the eyes that linger and ache" is looking down on him, and "shadow [l] y beckons" him with "thin pale hands." He falls asleep only to dream of the life he has led. In other words, his dream takes him down memory lane. He dreams running into a "desolate crowd" following a hearse in the rain. At a point the "coffin falls down and blocks the way," the corpse falls out of the coffin and stains the road with blood. A crowd of men and women standing by "murmur together, in voices not low nor loud, / Always the same stark words, slack-lipped and sore weeping from grinding pain! / On they stagger with hands a tremble and poor heads bowed." The sick man is seized with terror and when he awakens he turns to God in prayer. He realizes that the "monstrous corpse" of the dream is no other but his "bad soul" which needs to be cleansed. He turns around to look for the woman but she is already gone. He becomes aware that he is alone and that he has a very short time to live since "the hours sneer by, dragging with them the years." Obviously, the woman that stood at the foot of his bed represents a holy figure; she has come to guide him. He decides to follow her wherever she leads him. The poet selected this situation in order to describe the persona's last stage of purification and to remind the reader of the depth into which his soul wallowed. The defeat of the false self has been completed and the way to the gates of Heaven is now open.

In *The Veil of Light* the poet shows the persona after having ascended to Heaven. O'Sullivan depicts the persona in the act of looking down on the earth from above. "From this point whence the world looks far and deep, / We are triumphant on the earth's dull plain." Actually, the persona has completed his penance and that has qualified him to leave Purgatory behind. At last, after undergoing so many tribulations he is rewarded. He describes this new place as a location where all the winds "come to sleep" for there is no gust or gale but only peace and calm. The turbulence of the sea and the hardships he has encountered on his long journey all come to an end. He has finally obtained the desired reward that was "hardly won! But now this comely peace." Now he can have different dreams, dreams that mock life, strife, and all painful thoughts. His dreams will not be about earthly objects and situations; instead, they will be about heavenly joys. Now he has reached the position where he can see clearly how much vice there is among people and how much fear and terror permeates their hearts as they travel "down the valleys of the universe." He describes life on earth as a curse which man has to live with. As a matter of fact, man's life is viewed as nothing more than a sinister event. But life from above, as he presently sees it, is so different. He can see all things that are disguised, something he could not do when he was on earth. In the last stanza he considers himself one of the many children of God who along with them will "ride upon the wings of night." These children represent the souls of all those who succeeded in arriving to Heaven. As the poem nears its end the persona becomes conscious of the "veil of light" that blurs his vision of God. It is the only remaining obstacle that has to be overcome. He prays that the veil may be drawn so that he may see God's face. The ultimate union cannot take place if this "hard, intolerable Veil of light" is not pulled away. He is very close to God now, but he still needs to continue to pray and prove himself to his Father. The final epiphany is not far away. The soul that is in a state of grace stands already in the antechamber of Heaven and is separated only by the thinnest of veils from the face of God. When this veil is worn thinner and thinner until it disappears altogether and "the supernatural life of the soul increases," the presence of God will take on a new form. God will then penetrate the soul more intimately. He will be known in the full brilliancy of the Light of glory.[91]

The veil is man's mortality, his physical existence that stands between him and his Lord; it is this veil that has to be removed. The persona has at last emerged from the land of darkness, that unfortunate region, where the inhabitants sit in the shadow of death, where destruction passes for propagation, and a thick black night covers the glorious spring day. Theologians argue that when all the fruits of the world have turned to dust and ashes in man's mouth then man will be driven, exhausted, into the bosom of Abraham. Similarly, Jesus preached about self-denial and redemption when he told his disciples, "if any man will come after me, let him deny himself, and take up his cross, and follow me. For whosoever will save his life shall lose it; and whosoever will lose his life for my sake shall find it" (*Matthew* 16.24-25).

To help the reader realize that the heavenly state is a lot more valuable to man as well as convey the idea of futility O'Sullivan wrote *Memento Homo Quia Pulvis Es*. In the poem the poet emphasizes the idea that all will turn to "ashes" and to "dust," in order to prove that the material life is not worth clinging to. In a "convent chapel" the "vesper cadences" travel all over the world as death is tolled. The melody of the organ is quelled by the voices of the choir. Death evokes different feelings to each worshipper who inadvertently represents people from all walks of life. "For the rich it throbs like a passing bell / It murmurs like soothing of soft sea-shell." The "scholar" dreams alone, the "nun" remains locked up in her "somber cell," the "madmen" mutter to themselves and, finally, "the hollow-eyed trulls with their souls to sell" shut their ears to the tolling bell for they do not want to be reminded of death. The devil watches closely the effect of the tolling bell on the different people and detects deep fear aroused in their heart. He tries very cunningly to persuade each man and woman to ignore the implication of the bell's sound. The devil is convinced that if man shuts his ears to the sound of the tolling bell, then he will forget death and, continue in his sinful ways. Actually, this is the first poem in which good and evil are seen engaged in a battle over the soul of man. The devil attempts desperately to seduce souls that have succeeded in breaking away and have reached very close to God's kingdom by asking them to shut their ears to the sound of the bell. The bell functions as a reminder and awakens the soul from its deep sleep. It is the bell that prompts the soul to set on its journey to discover the kingdom of God since it reminds man of the futility of earthly life. The persona then asks God if "this foul terror" will be quelled by death. The fear of eternal punishment makes every sinner tremble with fear. The question is, will fear make the sinner abandon his sinful lifestyle or will he wait until the worms eat up his "legs and bust." Will his skull "give forth this atrocious yell" of "ashes to ashes, dust to dust" when it is too late to do anything to save himself? The idea of temptation is once more implied in the poem as the poet argues that man has to find the strength to resist the devil's wiles and ignore his ways in order to continue on his destination. The Devil is desperately attempting to dissuade man to give up his desired goal. So while the repentant persona is attending mass in a chapel the devil asks him to shut his ears to the meaningful sounds of the bell's sound as he stands in the corner "laughing from the end of Hell."

O'Sullivan's poem echoes Hildegarde of Bingen's words in ***The Soul Afire*** when she says:

> O frail man! dust of the dust of the earth, ash of ashes, cry out and tell of the coming of pure salvation, so that those may be instructed who see into the very marrow of the scriptures and still will not proclaim or preach them because their blood is tepid and they are dulled to the cause of God.[32]

O'Sullivan concludes ***Poems*** by using the convention of the envoi. In the *Envoi* he states that this volume was never intended to entertain; instead, it was meant to delineate his own personal drama. The *Envoi* not only summarizes and concludes the collection it is also used by the poet to send a message to every one of his readers individually. The poet encourages each reader to identify with the persona's fears, doubts, and realizations, because then he will, be able to find a way out of the darkness and confusion of the *fin-de-siècle*. Maybe he, too, will decide to send his soul forth "to find some sweet pleasaunce." O'Sullivan ends where he began as he brings the persona's experience full round. He goes from the garden that is full of "writhing serpents" to the court of Heaven. A life of eternal joy and peace awaits each individual soul that decides to flee the earthly pain and abandon the physical condition. In this collection, the poet successfully presents his readers with an escape from the abyss and a blueprint for the redemption of their soul. He expresses a willingness to guide and help each one who listens to the tolling bell declaring the futility of earthly life. In this volume O'Sullivan depicts sin, repentance, and redemption, the major stages through which man's soul has to go if it is to attain the Holy marriage with the Divine.

At the end of the collection when O'Sullivan says that all turns to dust, there are mixed feelings of bitterness, disenchantment, and cynicism. It would have been different if the poet had ended his collection with a poem devoted to the desired union of the soul with the Divine. If the union had taken place then the feelings would have been those of ecstasy. In the final analysis, he cannot minimize the fact that his persona has succeeded in turning away from earthly beauty and the corruption of the flesh to heavenly beauty and the spirit. The soul that begins the journey is certainly different from the soul that arrives to the heavenly court. The soul at the end is the soul that dies along the way and is resurrected. It is the soul that is bigger than death because it is born of death. It is the soul that has cleansed itself of desires and passions. Finally, it is the soul that has saved itself and made it to the Court of Heaven.

The chapter concludes with the persona in Heaven's court and with a temporary satisfaction as to his achievement yet that is not enough, since his primary objective remains the assimilation with the Divine. It is true that the persona has found the way, and knows every step of it, but he needs to retake this arduous journey with the hope that this time it will lead to the Divine union. Obviously his soul needs some more purification. In the next chapter the reader will witness the descent of the soul to earth for the sole purpose of guiding and helping another sinful soul find the path to salvation. This act of love that the soul shows by sacrificing its own peace and happiness by returning to earth to lead sinful souls to Heaven's court helps purify itself still further. In addition, there is a need to test the knowledge and put into practice everything that has been learned. In the end the poet realizes that the best way to test the persona's resolve and find out the value of what he has acquired is to place him in the middle of the Houses of Sin.

Notes

Chapter II

[1] John of the Cross, ***The Dark Night of the Soul***, trans. Kurt F. Reinhardt (New York: Frederick Ungar Publishing Co., 1957)

[2] John of the Cross, ***The Dark Night of the Soul***.

[3] John of the Cross, ***Ascent to Mount Carmel in the Mount Carmel in The Dark Night of the Soul***, trans. Kurt F. Reinhardt (New York: Frederick Ungar Publishing Co., 1957) 19-20.

[4] James Finley, ***Merton's Palace of Nowhere: A Search for God through Awareness of the True Self*** (Notre Dame: Ave Maria Press, 1978) 31.

[5] Finley 34.

[6] Vincent O'Sullivan, ***Poems*** (London: Elkin Mathews, 1896). All citations are to this edition.

[7] Finley, ***Merton's Palace*** 54.

[8] R. W. Stott, ***Basic Christianity*** (London: Inter-Varsity,1973) 74.

[9] M. V. Kamath, ***Philososphy of Death and Dying*** (Pennsylvania: Honesdale Hamalayan International Institute, 1978) 117.

[10] Michel Quoist, ***Christ is Alive*** (Dublin: Gill and Macmillan, 1971).

[11] Saint Bonaventure, ***The Soul's Journey into God***, trans. Ewert Cousins (New York: Paulist Press, 1987) 53.

[12] Joan M.Ferrente, ***Woman as Image in Medieval Literature: From the Twelfth Century to Dante*** (New York: Columbia University Press, 1975) 131.

[13] Carl Jung, ***The Archetypes of the Collective Unconscious*** (New Jersey: Princeton University Press, 1968).

[14] Evelyn M. Simpson and George C. Potter eds., *The Sermons of John Donne* (Berkeley: Berkeley University Press, 1954) Vol. VII: 257.

[15] French Fogle, ed., *The Complete Poetry of Henry Vaughan* (New York: Anchor Books, 1964) 139.

[16] Thomas à Kempis, *Of the Imitation of Christ: Four Books* (Oxford: Oxford University Press, 1940) 175.

[17] A Kempis 176.

[18] A Kempis 118.

[19] Ernest de Selincourt ed., *The Poetical Works of William Wordsworth* (Oxford: Oxford University Press, 1988) 460.

[20] F. E. Hutchinson, ed., *The Works of George Herbert* (Oxford: Clarendon Press, 1967).

[21] Fogle, *Complete Poetry of Henry Vaughan* 140.

[22] Hutchinson, *Works of George Herbert* 153.

[23] Quiost, *Christ is Alive* 68.

[24] Saint Bonaventure, *The Soul's Journey into God* 58.

[25] George Walton Williams, ed., *The Complete Poetry of Richard Crashaw* (New York: Doubleday & Co., 1970) 65.

[26] F. C. Happold, *Mysticism: A Study and an Anthology* (London: Penguin, 1973) 59.

[27] A Kempis, *Of the Imitation of Christ* 81.

[28] E. Martin Stern & Bert Marino *Psychotheology: The Discovery of Sacredness in Humanity* (New York: Paulist Press, 1970) 32.

[29] M.V. Kamath, *Philosophy of Death and Dying* 55.

[30] Finley, *Merton's Palace of Nowhere* 34.

[31] Finley 128.

[32] Kelley, *The Fellowship of Saints* 125.

Chapter III
The Soul in God's Embrace

In *The Houses of Sin* Vincent O'Sullivan borrows the structure of the romance to portray the journey of the sinful soul from earth to God's embrace. The soul is shown visiting various places in its effort to find the right path that would lead it to redemption. Some of the places help the soul take a step forward, yet others cause it to retreat to the old sinful ways. Usually at the beginning of the journey the sinner is desperate and shows a weak resolve in taking the road to salvation because it demands many sacrifices. In addition, the sinful soul finds it hard to keep on track because it has lost the love and the grace of God by wallowing in sin for too long. Gradually real progress occurs. Throughout the journey the traveler becomes conscious that some change is underway. When the phase of hardships is over and the new reality sets in then the penitent finds himself in the court of Heaven ready for the ultimate union with the Divine.

Each poem in this volume is presented as an episode in a long epic that starts in Hell and ends in Heaven. At each stage the weak soul feels pain and despair because it finds it easier to fall back on its old ways. Sadly the sinner admits its weakness every time he fails, but by the end of the volume the sinner's soul is definitely different since it succeeds in overcoming its morose and apathetic state. The sinner also acknowledges his inability to do anything to free his soul from the physicality of the present. He also becomes conscious of the infernal situation he has created for himself by sinning. Eventually, the sinner realizes that he cannot save his soul without God's grace, so he turns to Christ for guidance. He is convinced that he should try to leave behind the state of Hell if he is to move to the next stage, that of Purgatory, where his soul will be further cleansed and prepared for its final abode in God's court. All the sinner has to do is decide to relinquish the sensual sinful world with all its temptations and pleasures. O'Sullivan describes the sinner as trapped in the web of sin and the world of darkness. Only if he finds the courage to disentangle himself from this web will he move not only forward, but also upward. After all, that seems to be the crux of the matter.

The main idea underlining the volume is the conflict between two forces. On the one hand, there is the force that pulls the sinner downward, when he is tempted by the attractive web, on the other, there is the force that pushes him upward in an attempt to help him climb out of the web. Not only does this experience ache it also fills him with fear and doubt since his spiritual salvation looms further out of reach if he fails. The metaphors and symbols the poet associates with the quest such as the pilgrimage to the house of light; the night journey through the land of darkness toward the East and sunrise; and the ascent sometimes guided by the saintly stars and sometimes through total blackness to Mount Carmel abound. The road described is long and arduous, and passes through desert and ravine, while after sunset the night birds hover and wail, the feral fires lead astray, and the storms rage. But having once glimpsed at the shining spires the sinner/pilgrim finds it difficult to stay and rest before he enters that shady city of the palm trees.

In **The Houses of Sin** (1897) the poet deals with two significant themes. First, the need the sinner feels to recognize and admit his weakness and wickedness as well as gauge the depth into which he has fallen; and second, to discover the height to which he can rise with the help of Divine grace. Both themes underlie the volume and are successfully dramatized by O'Sullivan in poem after poem. It should be remembered that the persona of the previous collection **Poems** returns to help and guide out of Hell a sinful soul. In the process, the already saved persona has the opportunity to identify with the sinful soul he plans to save and further cleanse himself. Moreover, having become one of God's knights he has a mission to fulfill and that is to save a sinful soul for God. O'Sullivan suggests that attaining peace and union with the Divine is not a one-time achievement; instead, it is an everlasting effort that has to be repeated over and over again. At first, the reader witnesses the nether world into which the sinful soul has fallen as a result of its evil ways, then he sees the sinner's admission of weak resolve, but also the stages he goes through to achieve atonement. Man has to accept Divine grace and find a way to put himself in the hands of God. Trust and faith will work together to cleanse his soul and free it from the shackles of the flesh that were responsible in throwing it into the nether world in the first place. Somehow one senses that the poet assumes the role of a preacher. It is as though the drama of the sinner is the poet's drama as well. Now that his soul has been redeemed he can set an example for whoever wishes to learn from his experience. Subsequently, writing for O'Sullivan acquires a therapeutic function and at the same time, a didactic aspect for those who read his poems. To the audience of the 1890's who believed fervently in the value of experience a sermon would not be as effective as this string of poems written under intense emotion. Like in the presence of a morality play the reader witnesses the soul's journey from Hell to Heaven and into God's embrace in the most symbolic manner. Unquestionably **The Houses of Sin** conveys a moral in an aesthetic way, as Walter Pater and Oscar Wilde would say, the only acceptable way to address the audience at that time.

The journey depicted in O'Sullivan's volume resembles that of **Everyman** and that of Christian in **Pilgrim's Progress**. The reader accompanies the sinner through trials and tribulations to final salvation. In **The Houses of Sin** the redeemed persona of **Poems** quests together with the sinner for the glorious Holy Grail, which in this case, and from the theological point of view, is none other but the union of the pure soul with God. O'Sullivan's poems are proof of how a poet of the Decadent period succeeded in turning his own personal drama into a universal one by means of aesthetics.

In the opening poem of the collection O'Sullivan refers to the futility of passion after the persona has succeeded in ascending to Heaven. What has remained behind is nothing more than "remnants of passion, remnants of defeat / Ye rags and motley of outworn desire." The saved soul realizes how foolish it has been to live in sin and to be filled with fear of both God and Satan alternatively. Since all his fears have turned to ashes, the persona realizes that he has been foolish to mourn for "worthless things of earth." Having relinquished everything physical the soul feels that it has succeeded in defeating these "bleak days of idle sin with madness shod" forever. The poet ends the poem by referring to the fire that will burn all matter and purify his soul still further. With this poem O'Sullivan intended to unite his two volumes thematically and attain continuity. As a matter of fact, he suggests that the futility of the physical is a basic idea with which to start this collection, while it happens to be the same idea that concluded the previous volume. That is why **The Houses of Sin** starts with Hell from which the sinner's soul will be seen setting on its quest in an attempt to cleanse itself. When the soul ascends to Purgatory it will pause to undergo more purification and when it is completely pure; then and only then, it will be sent off to unite with the Divine.

Remnants outlines the direction the volume follows as it moves from the temptations of the world and the torture of Hell to the final rebirth in Heaven. The anguish and the pain of suffering, the fear of being doomed in Hell forever as well as Purgatory where purification occurs and hope for salvation is inculcated, are depicted. The reader witnesses the presence of Hell in the first poem. O'Sullivan suggests indirectly that the restless world of the nineties resembled hell. This poem summarizes the basic experience the poet plans to depict in this volume. It also stresses the fact that it is only at the end of his life that the sinner becomes aware of the futility of his passions and fears.

> Bleak days of idle sin with madness shod,
> Wishes scarce wished before they had an end,
> The fear of Satan, and the fear of God,
> Now with the ashes blend.

It is always at the end that man realizes that throughout

his life his soul was caught up in the battle between God and Satan. It is only after man goes through the pleasures of the Houses of Sin, and the pain of punishment that he learns that salvation lies in his own hands. He learns that the two forces exemplified in the two "rivals" possess his soul. He has to discover all alone the strength of his goodness, and that is something he can do only by going through the web of evil. With the grace of God and faith in Christ's sacrifice, O'Sullivan's redeemed persona helps the sinner realize that it is possible to defeat the demon that strengthened the "false self." To redeem his soul the sinner has to follow Christ up the hill of Calvary. This volume consists of a series of episodes that form an organic whole. Like **Poems**, it refers to the vast and deep world of the human psyche. It is worth mentioning that the quest does not have only a psychological level but also a theological one since this internal drama is full of complex conflicts that occur between the two major rivals: God and Satan. The sinner certainly needs courage not only to confront the fearful, beastly shapes of his dark psyche, but also God's grace to defeat them.

Vincent O'Sullivan's second volume of poetry ***The Houses of Sin*** personifies a number of the deadly sins. In the first eponymous poem the poet presents the persona ready to travel through the Houses of Sin in search of the sinful soul he has to save. The sinner, therefore, will not be alone since he will have a guide to explain some of the things he will see on the way. The colors and descriptions that are used by O'Sullivan in his portrayal of the Houses of Sin were common and suggestive in the nineties. The light is "yellow" and the night is dark and misty when the sinner ventures out into the streets of the city looking for excitement. In the previous collection the reader witnessed the persona sending off his soul to find the heavenly Paradise. While here the poet sends his persona into the city to find the sinner who has gone out to relish the various pleasures provided by the Houses of Sin. In the first collection O'Sullivan stressed the soul while in this one he emphasizes the body. The poet believed that the soul has to go through the body if it wants to save itself. As has been mentioned in the previous chapter, the body is symbolized by the grave, and death is the means through which the sinner has to go before he liberates his soul. The poet enhances the scene sensually as he underlines the "laughter that sounded everywhere" and the "sweet persons [that] stood and gazed on Heaven's floor," as "perfumed wind c[a]me glancing by." The poet uses images that suggest that charm and temptation have instilled the air. The sinner appears depressed and expects to get a chance to lift his spirits on that night. His melancholic state makes him approach the source of a charming voice. Any change would be welcome because he yearns for escape from his present dark mood and "the horrid crew / Of daily tiresome deeds, the noisome crowd." So he accepts the invitation of a stranger who "soothed my loneliness." This stranger is no other than the redeemed persona of ***Poems*** that comes back to guide the sinner through the rough road of redemption.

The young sinner, like so many young men living during the *fin-de-siècle*, has had "strange disgrace / Settled in the morning of his years, / And bowed him to a life of shame and tears." Clearly, he is ashamed of his outrageous actions that is why he leaves his lodgings only at night. Even though he is ashamed he does not show any readiness to discontinue indulging in the eating of the "forbidden fruit;" something he means to do this night as well. His steps lead him to the various Houses of Sin, and as he arrives at the first house he discovers it is that of Avarice. He enters and notes an old dame sitting at a "wheel," spinning "gold threads," which she then uses to weave a web for the sole purpose of trapping human souls. Through the use of personification the poet succeeds in dramatizing the sins to the *fin-de-siècle* audience. This poem aims to expose some of the vices that prevailed during that period. As the sinner visits house after house he discovers how men are trapped. It was like seeing "wreckage cast up by one great shuddering sea."

The sinner then visits the house of Pride where he finds

a gracious hostess. Something about her eyes attracts his attention. He learns that whoever looks at her eyes goes on serving her until death. It was almost daybreak when his footsteps led him to the "dark sisters" Anger and Jealousy who "did their arms entwine." There he finds "a banquet of strange dishes outspread." And as he tastes a "subtle dish;" suddenly he feels he has no other wish in his heart. Gradually, he "grew as one asleep / Amongst the dead, whose passions strong and deep / Are merged in longed-for, unexpected peace, / And give them ease." Somehow the sinner ends up being trapped, he seems to be drugged and determined to stay in the house forever. At that time he notices a stranger, who is no other than the redeemed persona, lingering by and decides to invite him to taste of the "subtle dish" and to "join in this deathly feast and so make end." But the stranger replies that he is afraid to do so and instead, retires to a corner all by himself where he stands and weeps. The stranger is no other than the redeemed persona who has succeeded in saving his soul. He weeps because he feels sorry for the present sinner who in his despair fails to muster the courage to turn away from the world of sin.

In the Old Testament there are many examples wherein prophets point out that the will of God sometimes has to be done by destroying everything else. It seems that the cup of sin has to be drained to the lees before the resurrection process begins. Man finds it, sometimes, hard to understand the detours along which God takes him, and only much later does he see that he had to travel one way or another. O'Sullivan's view coincides with that of Thomas à Kempis who says:

> Temptations are often very profitable to us, though they be troublesome and grievous; for in them a man is humbled, purified, and instructed. All the saints passed through many tribulations and temptations, and profited thereby. There is no man that is altogether free from temptations whilst he liveth on earth; for in ourselves is the root thereof, being born with inclination to evil. The beginning of all evil temptations is

inconstancy of mind, and small confidence in God. For a ship without a helm is tossed to and fro with the waves so the man who is remiss and apt to leave his purpose, is many ways tempted. We know not oftentimes what we are able to do, but temptations do shew us what we are.[2]

It should be remembered that "death is the end of all, and man's life suddenly passeth away like a shadow." And à Kempis thought it was his duty to warn man and using Saint Luke's argument he says:

Think on nothing but the salvation of thy soul, care for nothing but the things of God, and Make new friends to thyself by honoring the Saints of God, and imitating their actions, that when thou failest in this life, they may receive thee into everlasting habitations. Keep thyself as a stranger and pilgrim upon the earth and one to whom the affairs of this world do nothing appertain.[3]

The idea of temptation as beneficent in the progress of the soul and in association with the concept of *felix culpa* is described in John Milton's **Paradise Lost** in the following lines:

> O goodness infinite, goodness immense
> That all this good of evil shall produce,
> And evil turn to good; more wonderful
> Than that which by creation first brought forth
> Light out of darkness; full of doubt I stand,
> Whether I should repent me now of sin
> By me done and occasioned, or rejoice
> Much more, that much more good thereof shall
>   spring,
> To God more glory, more good will to Man
> From God and over wrath grace shall abound.
>   **Paradise Lost**, XI, 468-478.[4]

The Houses of Sin are introduced to the reader as a passage to the world of death. Furthermore, the festive atmosphere the poet describes alludes to the feast of death where the skeletons are seen mocking the living. In this context the theme of death is overtly stressed. The question that arises in the sinner's mind is whether he can find the courage to escape from the banquet and take the trip to the underworld? Again, like in the previous volume the body of man is sent off to the kingdom of death so as to liberate the soul and, consequently, send it off to heaven. But "the pilgrim has also to fear the recalcitrance of the habitual self." The main enemies are principally the desires of the flesh and vain fears that arise in man's heart because human nature is corrupt. But more dreadful than the night around man are the death and darkness that lie within him.[5]

In *Malaria* O'Sullivan uses the theme of sickness. The persona witnesses the sinner who is stricken by malaria lying in bed thinking of death since all that comes to his mind is "Miasma spread like perfumed palls." And even though this is a macabre scene, the poet describes it sensually by referring to colors and fragrances. The situation the poet depicts occurs in the late evening after sunset.

> A violet and yellow flush
> Floats to intense skies like a spire:
> It bathes my heat with secret hush
> And fills my brain with dreaming fire.

The woman referred to in the poem is no other but the personification of sickness that seems, at this stage, very attractive to the indisposed man. She is viewed and described by him as a goddess. The "cool bed" he yearns to lie in is no other than the grave, and it happens to be the place where he wants to join the goddess of death. Sickness appears as the "harbinger of death." It is as though the "subtle dish" he ate from in the previous poem has made him sick. Obviously, the poet is not describing any physical ailment instead, he is alluding to a spiritual sickness of which the sinner is suffering. He has figured out that his soul is so sick that there is no other way out but death. Yet there seems to be no sign of regret. The "subtle dish" the sinner tasted has led him to a state of existence that is no different from that of death. It should not be forgotten that the feast he attended was the feast of the dead, an event that foreshadows his own death even though he was not aware of that at the time. The poem begins with sunset symbolizing the end of a day hence implying the end of the sinner's life. In the second stanza the poet distinguishes between the body and the soul. He knows that whenever he loses control over his body his soul will be set free. No wonder then the miasma of his body is a desired state since without it the soul will never have the opportunity to experience Heaven. Obviously, death becomes the only desired condition through which relief can be attained, first from the physical illness and second, from the body's dictates.

In *The House of the Ghosts* the sinner falls deeper and deeper into the abyss and encounters ghosts whose "earth-worn faces" shake him up. These ghosts rise "seeking each other's looks," and "strive to touch each other." The ghosts yearn to be alive again and as they look around them they notice what they possessed in the past. The sinner's narration refers to one of the ghosts who could not bear his miserable life and decided to end it by hanging himself. After his act was completed he remembers how his wife sobbed when she saw him "void of life." But presently his wife is happy and going on with her life while he is spending his nights alone. The ghosts "make converse in their woe" until daybreak when they have to return to their graves. In this poem O'Sullivan uses the supernatural element but does not refer to fairies as he did in the previous volume, instead, he refers to ghosts. He also envisioned the world of the fairies and that of the ghosts as distinct from each other. The world of the fairies lies above the earth, but that of the ghosts below. The fairies come to earth from a world that exists somewhere above while the ghosts come roaming from the grave. The fairies have no identity while the ghosts have, since before their death they lived under a name in the world. The fairies are happy and colorful while the ghosts are morose and pale. It is safe to assume that the sick man of the previous poem has turned into a ghost now that he is dead. He is listening to the story of another ghost who admits that he could not go on leading a miserable life and so committed suicide. O'Sullivan describes two different ways of entering the kingdom of death. The first way requires man to lie passively in his bed and wait for the end while the second, forces him to choose to terminate his life and enter the world of death sooner. The first ghost seems to have lacked the courage to achieve the salvation he yearned for as opposed to the second who fearlessly plunged headlong into darkness to obtain his wish. But the second ghost seems to have regretted leaving behind all his material possessions and his wife. Now "behind those lit windows she delights," and he "must lie here till the end of nights / Listening to the dull throbs / Of the sea." The sinner then goes on to compare his past life with his present saying: "I thought that life beneath the sun was hard, that to lie here were peace." It is obvious that O'Sullivan is condemning the act of suicide that may be an easy way out of the painful life man has to endure on earth. Terminating one's life happened to be the common way with many of the young men in the nineties. Through this poem the poet attempted to suggest that man should bear his suffering patiently until the time comes for him to leave the world. The slow, tedious process seems to be better than the quick way out.

In *The Verge* O'Sullivan depicts a man on the verge of another state. The poem postulates life on the verge between the present and the future, on the verge between life on earth and life beyond it, and on the verge of how things are and how they ought to be. The sinner is alone in a dark chamber contemplating on what his life has been. For the first time he feels remorse for sinning, and admits his mistakes even though he does not show any signs of repentance yet. The "ancient clock" strikes twelve and is compared to a bell tolling his death. Every stroke sends a shudder through his heart and as he is violently shaken he awakens from his drowsiness and faces the "glamour of approaching death." In the next few lines, he describes a "sheeted ghost whose face is hid." The ghost will haunt him for a long time to come since he does not seem to be able to forget "its strange pallor, what its grace," and wonders how it will feel "when the unveiling doth take place," and he looks straight at it. The sinner expresses the wish to hear from the ghost about the various places it has been, and hopes that the ghost might answer some of the questions he has about the world beyond this one.

> Ah, at the midnight one man tries
> To gather near, to lift the veil
> And read upon that face its tale;
> To gather near that dread and holy
> Figure, and his melancholy
> Shatter by a wild caress
> In all sombre silentness.

Once the veil is thrust aside a pale, compassionate female face is revealed to the sinner. She "seeks for his face and kisses him" and, suddenly, all the shadows that have haunted him "writhe" and vanish. He remembers her "glorious hair" and how beautiful she used to be in the past. Now there is pallor to her face but also a certain serenity that enhances her beauty. Now she is no more but "a filmy figure, almost air." When the figure appears, the sinner refers to "blinding clouds" interfering with his vision. The sinner realizes the reality of his condition and decides to cross the dividing line to start a new life. The "flying shrouds" and the "shadows that fall" are a sign that he has made this crossing. The sinner's mood changes from sad, at the beginning of the poem, to joyful at the end. After midnight the sinner will be in a different world. The union that takes place at the end of the poem is between the sinner and the beautiful figure of Death that has come to claim him. "The sacred figure, grave and dim, / Seeks for his face and kisses him."

In *Drug* O'Sullivan wished to depict the England of the *fin-de-siècle*. As the sinner continues his lonely walk down the streets of the city his attention is drawn to the "pale-eyed men [that] take stand and glare / Upon the sin-soiled floor of

Picadilly." And "the harlots of the pavement fling their silly / Maniac laughter in their great despair." What he sees depresses him immensely so he decides to take a drug that will "light up the dusty caverns of my soul," and maybe will help him understand a great deal. This drug leads him to a world where he inhabits with his beloved locked up in an embrace. O'Sullivan is examining the possible escape that drugs can offer as he has done with suicide earlier. Drugs were one of the many options available to the young men of the nineties with which they experimented. The question is whether drugs could lead to a lasting escape from the hardships of life, or whether it was only a temporary solution. What kind of world does the young man find himself in after the drug wears of? Is the world any different? The drug does offer the persona a sensual world, a colorful reality which is scary because it is crowded with ghosts. The reality he returns to is totally different, and the shock after noticing the difference between the two kinds of reality unbearable. The pain increases and the young man can only welcome the "sweet drug" again and again until the end of time, because it "lights up the dead oppressive days, and shines Miraculous life-giver."

In *Three Moments* the poet divides his poem into three parts in which the drama of the lover unravels. The lover is present in all three parts. In the beginning, the lover is seen in his garden during the night waiting for the "Queen of Love" to come to him. He wants the stars to lighten up the night and the nightingales to sing sweetly. The woman he is in love with is very important to him because, as he says, "she perfumes my dreams" and her "soul lights my soul with its beams." He is confident that she will come to him that night and with "the passion her purities bring" will change him too. Somehow her coming will change his life forever because she represents an escape from his misery.

In the second part, the reader witnesses the beloved with her husband. She confesses that she has sinned with another man in order to give him fame and power because that is the only way she could give him pleasure. But she promises not to "swerve / No whit, not be shaken: / You I serve." She goes on to refer to her lover as a "madman," and a "foolish lad" and wonders how she could ever have loved him. She suggests that her lover tried to trap her but all he succeeded in doing was "forge his own fetters." Now he sits alone waiting for her but she does not plan to see him again because, as she claims, she loves only her husband. And when she departs she quietly utters "this is death" for she senses that the end is very near. As a matter of fact, she senses the dangerous situation she has placed herself in.

In the third part of the poem the scene shifts back to the lover who is still waiting for the "Queen of Love" to appear. It is clear that he has waited for a very long time since the garden that was covered with the scent of blooming flowers is now covered with snow. While playing with one of her gloves, given to him as a memento of their love, it dawns on him that he has been deceived. And "Sudden I found my playing was in vain," and that "she wronged me and she crushed me to despair / That woman with the lustful raven hair." Filled with frustration and anger, he "seize [s] a poisoned knife and [strikes] her dead" the moment she arrives. Killing the beloved is interpreted as killing his "false self" which eventually will burn in the fires of Hell until it is purified. This act reminds the reader of her prediction that the end had come. The sinner goes on to describe her as a Medusa because of her three heads that are now enclosed in three coffins. It is said that she had a head for herself, a second for her husband, and a third for her lover. The beloved is depicted as a woman who took on different disguises in order to deceive men. The beloved is also presented as a monstrous creature and that symbolizes the false self of the sinner. Actually, the attractive "Queen of Love" proves by her actions that she is a witch. Now that she is dead her "magic kiss" will "stir the damp worms as they prey and hiss." The symbolic level of the poem refers to the sinner who feels somewhat relieved for having eliminated his "false self" implied by the beloved's death. Yet the sinner believes that his soul will have to burn "in the torment of God's hell." The natural landscape in which the lover rejoiced at the beginning now turns into a scary landscape which he abhors and fears. Earth gives way to Hell and it is only a matter of time before he relinquishes the first for the latter. And yet, even though he has "forged his fetters" by living a life of sin and deceit; it is not too late to seek death. He is tortured with confusion and fear. He has to give up the joyful garden and the song of the nightingale for the cold world of loneliness where the growling of wolves as well as moans and groans are the only sounds that are carried, by the wind, to his ears. The once beautiful world is now a macabre and eerie one.

Love in Tears picks up where the last poem left off as the lover visits the grave of his dead beloved. He bends his "melancholy head" "down among the grasses of the grave" and "for [his] dead love did sadly crave." Time has gone by and he has come to forgive her for what she has done to him. Furthermore, he expresses a wish for the peace she is enjoying and hopes that he, too, will be relieved of his anguish. An "idle maid" who is watching shows sympathy for him. The lover hopes his beloved will set him free for he feels his punishment is no other but her grasp on him. The idle maid bends over and touches his hair and then passes away. O'Sullivan says: "Quickly unto the grayish lichened seat / And sat there moping: clouds were in her eyes, / As one who dreams a space or yet she dies." And by the end of the poem the sinner is seen leaving the graveyard together with the idle maid who is no other than the resurrected beloved/soul that has returned from the underworld. Bending his head on the grave earlier is a symbolic act since it foreshadows the union that will occur by the end of the poem. All along they wished for this union and now the time is ripe for that. Love and temptation are the means that link life with death. The image of the dead beloved/soul is conveyed by the poet when the persona remembers how "her mellow hair still wave / And laugh and glitter like the morning sea, / As when in old lost days it played with me." It is clear, therefore, that the dead woman and the idle maid are one and the same. This is the first poem of the volume in which O'Sullivan uses the theme of the dead beloved to suggest the two states of the sinner's soul: past innocence and present sinfulness. Finally, the repentant sinner identifies with the beloved/soul that has been through death and the grave and has now arisen.

The Dancer at the Opera depicts a dancer who has the face of "a holy nun," but a soul "drunken with the vaunts / She tolled, like maddened bee, from lips / That gave her wondrous body chaunts." The dancer represents the two selves, the true and the false, in the human soul. This poem is also divided into three parts where the dual personality of the dancer is given in the first part. In the second part she prepares herself to get more "triumph," but is faced with her own coffin, and symbolically, the death of her soul which sends her trembling to the confessional. In the last part of the poem the poet describes the King watching over the repentant dancer as the "harp-notes" continue to convey "the devil's dirge." On the one hand, the poet shows that the devil has lost the battle over the dancer's soul while on the other, God is portrayed as the winner since the dancer's soul has been saved. The dancer has "ceased to sin" because fear of damnation has prompted her to change her lifestyle. She repents and is redeemed. Furthermore, the poet describes the dancer as having "calm eyes and mystic grace," which means that even though she sinned she never lost the grace of God completely. When she decides to go out that evening, it is vespers time and the common folk are kneeling "before the crucifix" and saying their "Hail Marys." She encounters the "Four men of grave and sombre mien / Four men in funeral array bearing a coffin" which happens to be her own. The undertaker says: "We bring this coffin here for a / Mademoiselle who died today; / The dancer at the opera." She finds it hard to believe him and so draws the "sable bands" aside and discovers that her name is on it. In shock she runs out into the street and starts looking for a church to confess her sins instead of a "garish hall" to indulge in sensuous pleasures.

In this poem O'Sullivan describes the dancer as torn

between two lives of which she has been trying to choose for some time. The time has come to choose between a life of sensuality and a life of spirituality. The dancer, like any enlightened soul, abandons the former for the latter and retires to a convent to continue her life with the "gray-clad holy nuns." The poet suggests that even though the dancer's false self enjoyed living a profane life the true self finally overcomes and good prevails. Without question, all depends on man's will to shed sin and save his soul. The active way is stressed in this poem. Earthly life is perishable, crude, and weak, while heavenly life is imperishable, glorious, and powerful. Somehow the one is an extension or development of the other. Obviously, the motion is not from a higher state of life to a lower one but the opposite. The motion is upward since with death man moves to a higher not a lower plane of existence. The following words ring a bell:

> Listen, and I will tell you a secret. We shall not all die, but suddenly, in the twinkling of an eye, every one of us will be changed as the trumpet sounds! The trumpet will sound and the dead shall be raised beyond the reach of corruption, and we then who are still alive shall suddenly be utterly changed. For this perishable nature of ours must be wrapped in imperishability.[6]

This is exactly what happens to the dancer who seems to be reborn out of the ashes of her own corrupt life. From the dead soul enclosed in the coffin springs finally a new and different one, the true self comes to life from the remains of the false self.

In *Woman of the Mist* O'Sullivan describes the sinner all alone on a wet rainy evening. He wishes for the company of a woman to cheer him up. He discerns with difficulty a woman coming toward him. For the first time in this collection the sinner is seen wandering along the shore looking out to the sea and yearning for the woman of the mist to appear. Suddenly the poet reveals that she is not alive and that she may be another ghost. The woman the sinner imagines seeing turns out to be only a spirit by the end of the poem. The symbolism of the sea as the grave is implied, as for the spirit it is no other than that of death. In this way his desire to see the ghost suggests his wish to die. "Dear love, hear the thudding drums / Heralding the death that comes / To entreat me with his smile." Finally, he is assured that the woman of the mist is no other than a spirit that cannot be seen or held. It is clear that the form the wanderer gives her is all a product of his vivid imagination since

> With empty eyes and vacancy
> I watch the dull and crying sea,
> And linger on the hard wild shore
> For one who comes no more no more.

In the next poem *Shadows,* the poet unravels the same idea but this time within a different landscape. The "passionate flowers" lose their wildness and color since dawn and the bees "tumble." Every single place seems to have been visited by ghosts. Everything has changed for the sinner so when he looks around him all he can see is ghosts and shadows. The question that ensues is whether this is the way the sinner envisions the newfound reality. Certainly, he has found a different world but is unable to describe it because it is still muddled in his mind. In the following poems O'Sullivan tries to answer the question about the new reality. The fact that the sinner sees shadows and ghosts shows that he has reached a new state of existence. This is the same state that appeared on the opposite shore in *Woman of the Mist.* It is evident that the sinner seems to have left behind one state that of Hell and has moved to another that of Purgatory. Obviously it is the purification of his soul that has made him see these shadowy figures which he cannot discern yet, and therefore, is unable to describe them.

In *The Children of Wrath* O'Sullivan uses the child for the first time in this volume. But the child is not presented as innocent because it has already learned about the sin of wrath. In this poem the sinner arrives at the gates of Hell where he meets the devil. The devil is described as sitting in a "herbless plain," a sterile land, a "desert." He is surrounded by his courtiers who are a "throng of souls in pain." It is a scary place where "wild lightning" breaks out and instead of birds chirruping he hears ravens croaking. The sinner addresses the devil as "Almighty Master, thou whose name is feared / Throughout the sick world, and whose heart is cheered / By suitors, why alone?" The devil leers and replies that if he were to look around he would not see a single human footprint in this wild desert that surrounds him. The sinner kneels before the master of darkness and pays homage to him. The devil suggests that the sinner might as well start walking around praising God and blaspheming the devil in order to fool everyone who hears him; that he says, would work to his advantage. Actually, the devil is asking the sinner to behave hypocritically. Interestingly, the devil admits that whoever has the Holy Spirit in his soul is reminded of the fact that the "fire of Hell" remains "alight." It seems only natural that a man whose soul is governed by the Holy Spirit will always fear the fires of Hell. In this way O'Sullivan undermines the power of the devil. It is only by the end of the poem that the reader discovers that the sinner, with the help of the redeemed persona that has been guiding him, has been putting up an act in order to fool the devil into liberating the lost souls from being "scorched and seared." This is a poem about hypocrisy and wrath two of the sins that the sinner encounters in the Houses of Sin. At the same time, it is one more poem wherein the reader sees the sinner, finally, choosing the active way as he plunges headlong on a collision course with the devil. He challenges the devil by using flattery when he addresses it, and uses guile in order to save other souls. The sinner is made to believe that man has the power to save himself as well as others from the clutches of the devil. Again, the poet notes that the existence of good and God's grace can enable man to achieve salvation and then become a guide to save others. Before leaving Hell the sinner, who has gone through multiple hardships, decides to lead the children of wrath out of their misery. Of course, this cannot be achieved before convincing

Satan to let them go. At this moment the redeemed persona inspires the sinner to disguise himself and appear as the Knight of God trying to win a lost soul for his King by using one of the devil's methods, that of deception, to achieve his goal. The battle does not end in this poem which means that the sinner has to continue fighting with the king of Hell. Tournier says, "Satan makes use of God's laws. He makes use of our instincts given to us by God to guide us toward goodness and happiness, and turns them into instruments of evil and misfortune."[6] And Finley's words shed light on O'Sullivan's argument when he says: "We are called upon to live Christ's life. We are called into the desert to meet the demon within. We are called to face God alone in the night of our own solitude. We are called to die with Jesus, in order to live with Him."[7]

Fear at Night continues to develop the same theme O'Sullivan presented in the previous poem. It is a cold and pale night where nature is first personified and then described as a wailing woman. As for the river it, too, is heard crying. The sinner feels that there is a "thing" or a ghost following him in order that he may be scared away, and most importantly, forget his mission of saving the children. The spirit is seen

> ... exploring the ground
> All night while dark winds rave,
> And heap a little mound
> It has a corpse to save
> It digs a shallow grave.

Instead of running away the sinner decides to confront the spirit. The confrontation is an admission of the kind of life he has led and which drove his soul to Hell. He also sees the ghost trying to dig a grave to hide a corpse. The sinner is determined to grab this spirit and "see it face to face" so he can make it go away. This "thing" which the sinner wants to stand up to is no other than the devil that is trying so hard to hold on to his soul. The redeemed persona can hear the penitent crying out for help "like a sick child" as his soul is being tormented in the underworld. He hopes that God can help hush the wailing soul. Finally, the persona wonders if he has been dreaming about the lost, tortured soul that is out there raving desperately.

> The specter in the corpse represents the high judge within ourselves who keeps record of everything, and in deep wisdom foreshadows all. We must become masters over the terrible world of the spirits, for they are within us as well as without. Whatever lies outside us which might be insignificant or unrelated to our mind and heart actually reflects and mirrors our inner self. This is what we should learn. And we are meant to approach through this way of learning to the ultimate, the last and highest possible realization the realization vouchsafed in the end: that of our divine identity with the substance, the consciousness, and the bliss that we know as God. This is the realization of the absolute nature of the Self. This is the discovery of the jewel at the core. We also learn that all the "thous" of our surrounding night and day are disguises, masks and playful self-duplications of the Self of the world. This is the awakening of joy.[8]

Our Lady of the Fields is a poem about the Blessed Virgin Mary. During the night when everybody is asleep in the small village on the hill, the Virgin is seen walking through "the flocks of sheep." As the Virgin passes over the fields she blesses the harvest. The persona refers to the small churchyard and the numberless children that lie there. The Virgin is seen by some villagers, leading "a good dead child." At the same time, the persona refers to the penitent sinner who is also in deep need of help, and who eventually turns to the Virgin Mary. This is the first poem in the volume that deals with the Holy Virgin. She is seen leading a child away from death and the graveyard. The persona also views the repentant sinner

-150-

praying desperately asking for protection from the wiles of the "old Man" who has been lingering ready to trap him and divest him of his determination and as such make him return to sin.

> Mary my mother
> Please cure me of the Old Man's spell,
> Which leads me down the road to Hell
> O Mary mother!

The persona narrates how the penitent sinner confesses "proud sins have my life undone" by "forcing me thy grace to shun." As a result, the penitent soul has found itself in the abyss lost, desperate, and alone. He hopes that the Virgin Mary will see him as she has seen the "good dead child." He yearns for the Virgin's look which is going to help him return to grace. The image of the child symbolizes the sinner's soul presently lying in the grave or the abyss. As a matter of fact, the persona wishes the Virgin to lead the sinner's soul out of the grave, that is, help in its resurrection.

The woman O'Sullivan describes in *Francis Borgia at Grenada* was beautiful and attractive to many men when she was alive. But now her "gracious form" has been "struck with a great paralysis" and she "cannot seek her resting place." When she died she was left to the slaves to carry her to church. Before her death there were other changes as well. Her hair "dwindled into dross" and her "cheeks which striving roses sought to vie, / Are still and hard as clay becomes with cold." Time and illness have brought about changes on the beautiful queen who was once so attractive and desirable. In addition, the poet refers also to the power she held for she "swayed cities and lives of men," and was ruler of many lands. Presently she has lost all the power she possessed and rules nothing, not even the coffin she inhabits.

The poet alludes to the true story of Francis Borgia, a Spanish nobleman whose attitude changed after he stood guard to Queen Isabella's bier. The incident made him realize the futility of life and prompted him to withdraw from the activities of the court in order to pursue a hermit's life.

O'Sullivan describes the guard who was appointed to stand by the queen's coffin and exposes the thoughts that went through his mind. The sinner wonders if the deceased ever believed in God and, at the same time, refers to a poor old man who pressed the crucifix to his breast when he died. According to the sinner's reasoning all potentates differ from common men because they stop being loyal to God. They seem to forget that their crown is good on earth and not in heaven. Similarly, God allows them to act out their role for a while in the same way other people do and when it is time they, too, have to go like the rest. The vanity of man is limitless so when the end comes he can hardly realize that material possessions as well as his power are insignificant. O'Sullivan uses the image of the world being a stage on which "we play our parts." That stage, says the poet, is no other than God's "outstretched hand." On it man is permitted to continue to act until God decides to "close His hand" bringing about the end. In addition, the poet deals, in this poem, with the theme of transience specifically in reference to beauty and youth. The bitter realization that time cannot be subjected is acknowledged by all men whether these are powerful rulers or just common subjects. In the poem the poet describes the queen in the past when she was young and beautiful, as well as in the present as an invalid, old, and ugly. Then the poet goes on to suggest both the brevity of life and the futility of the world. The metaphor of the woman who was beautiful then became ugly and finally died, is used by the poet to show the sinner's soul that deteriorated through sin until it died. Eventually, the sinner has to find a way to rediscover his soul. He has to take action before it is too late. One thing is certain, though, the sinner has accepted the idea of death as the only means of rebirth.

In *Calvary Hill* O'Sullivan chooses to write about a Biblical event in relation to the experience of his sinner. As Christ went up Calvary so does the sinner, but there is a difference between them. The former never doubted His footsteps up the hill, while the latter, is incessantly afraid that he will slip and fall. The penitent sinner continues to be vulnerable to sin and temptation and so prays for Christ's protection. He implies that the devil is watching him closely, waiting for him to lower his guard so he can attack. But the one figure who seems to be the most dangerous of all is "Saul of the gibing mouth." In the second stanza the poet refers to the birth of Christ a joyous event, which juxtaposes the painful experience at hand, that of climbing Calvary foreshadowing His death, an event that prompted immeasurable sorrow. The two events form the beginning and the end of Christ's life. They are two different events with different implications and evocative of powerful emotions. At this point, the persona witnesses the penitent sinner beginning to sigh under the burden of his cross. As a matter of fact, the sinner has to understand that he will not have to physically die. All that is expected of him is cleansing his soul and eliminating sin from it completely giving himself the opportunity to be saved by the sacrifice of Christ. The sinner has to persist in climbing this hill, and at the same time, he has got to continue to resist the wiles of the devil. The redeemed persona refers to the sinner's soul that was innocent and pure when it came to earth as well as how it became sinful. The poet outlines the motion of ascendance and the moment of pain in Christ's life as well as the altruistic love that Christ has shown in dying for mankind. It is only in the last stanza that the reader discovers that the time the poet is writing the poem is Christmas. Thus the poet intentionally juxtaposes the happiness associated with Christ's nativity with His sad death in the first stanza of the poem. It is "Yule night" and the sinner wishes that Christ will look in his direction as He looked on the innocent sheep that gathered around Him on that cold night when He lay in the manger. The penitent sinner is convinced that he needs protection from "the elf-man and each evil wight / Who prowls about us while we sleep." He wants Christ to shield him "from wily ruse / Of ghosts who bring the mists from south." The allusion of evil residing in the south refers to the idea that Hell was supposed to be situated south of the earth. It was also believed that the Christian Heaven was situated above that is, north of the earth. The notion of Heaven that prevailed was that it was a completely spiritual and anti-material place. The earth existed in the middle, that is, south of Heaven and north of Hell and was thought as a place of trial and tribulation while Hell was the dreaded realm of retribution for wrong behavior. The poem signals the turning point in the collection as the sinner decides to climb Calvary Hill and follow in Christ's footsteps.

The sinner has come to know that the path through the vale of sin and death is a road of trials, and that his guide will lead him through the wilderness, through sea, sand, and serpents. Yet, he has acquired enough courage and determination not to be scared. He has decided not to let anything stop him from attaining Jerusalem. "The journey is also dangerous because at every turn the world, the flesh, and the devil may proffer of their good, beckoning onto the broad and pleasant-seeming primrose path."[9]

Jesus said that He was the way, the truth, the life, that no one went to the Father except through Him, that whoever saw him saw the Father, and that the Father was in Him and He in the Father. It is known that Jesus came to save the world, and so without Him there can be no salvation for man. Consequently whoever separates himself from Christ loses sight of Him, separates himself from God, and turns his back on salvation. Moreover, whoever turns his back on Christ turns away from the opportunity given to him for his own full development and the acquisition of a better world.

The mystery of the Redemption, says Quoist, is also the mystery of the Resurrection since the Way of the cross does not end at the tomb but continues beyond death and leads to the joy of eternal life. "Jesus is the great conqueror of sin, suffering, and death. In Christ every man and all of mankind, whether in the past, present, or future, are dead and brought to life again."[10] In the Bible we are told that "God brought us to life with Christ. It is through grace that you have been saved. He raised us up with him and gave us a place with him in Heaven, in Christ" (*Epheseus* 2. 5-6).

O'Sullivan's poetry is living evidence of these views.

Undoubtedly, he believed that a Christian in his daily life must freely embark with Jesus on that unique and total Passion. If the Christian dies to himself every day, he will attain life, true life, an expanded life because selfishness will disappear, because he will be transfigured by death, divinized by love, and made eternal. "At the end of our life on earth, when we die the final death of a series of deaths, we will have the most beautiful and complete opportunity to live in Jesus, the mystery of Redemption." Naturally death becomes the final stage in our development, "the final step in our climb toward transfiguration, the ultimate liberation from our limitations so that we may emerge into immortal life."[11]

O'Sullivan's poetry shows that the Redemption of Christ is not only a struggle and a victory over sin, but also "a struggle and a victory over suffering and death, over that suffering and death that Jesus Christ grasped, took to himself, and dynamized by means of his infinite love." Quoist attempted to explicate his argument by saying that "acknowledging our sins and giving them to the Father, in Christ the Saviour" is not enough. To achieve salvation we must be "willing to participate also in the struggle, which is the second aspect of the unique act of salvation," actively and fully.[12]

Hymn to May is a prayer offered to the Holy Virgin to whom the sinner turns for help. In this poem O'Sullivan centers his attention on the Mother of Christ. Her power of love for sinners is known and so the sinner expresses the wish to be purged by joining "the crowd" of redeemed souls when Jesus arrives. He hopes that she will listen to

> ... my illness to thee
> Of the illness which mocks,
> Which gibes with town-clocks,
> Till Death the gate locks.

Very quickly the sinner's wish becomes a decision to join the "throng" of the redeemed, and "with Him, my race run." It is spring and nature is blooming and happy. The Holy Virgin ventures forth, and at this moment all the "poor souls" see Her coming and crowd "round with their bowls," to "catch the light dew / Which falls from thy hair." This is his only chance to purify his soul and save himself. If the Holy Virgin comes to his help she will cure him of his "illness" which, in his case, is not physical but spiritual. He wants to be ready when "in a cloud / Comes Thy son" and becomes "one with the crowd."

In *At the Gate of the Year* the poet presents the penitent sinner in the process of reminiscing. And even though another year has gone by nothing of essence has happened. Readily he expresses his gladness that this year has come to an end. He personifies and then describes the year as passing away and heading toward the sea. He wishes that the New Year will be better and that Christ, his friend, will look on him more favorably. He adds that he hopes to be with his friend, but wonders if that will happen any time soon or if that meeting will take place before his death. This poem links death and birth, the beginning and the end. It is clear that there can be no beginning without an end since life springs from death. That is why the penitent sinner chooses to speak of the old year as heading toward the sea, the symbol of death and the grave but also, ritualistically, the source of rebirth and purification. He hopes that the New Year will bring the rebirth of his soul and that Christ will look on him again as He used to in the past. "Sweet friend of friends" he exclaims, "will your face look on mine again?" And in the next stanza "heart of my heart, shall we two meet," and finally, "soul of my life, shall I be dead / Ere you will kiss mine eyes again?" It is clear that the only thing the penitent sinner is thinking of is the union of his soul with Christ. As a matter of fact, he is trying to prepare as best he can for that event. Finally, the sinner hopes that the end of the year will take away his "false self," his sinful self and that during the New Year his soul will be reborn. The New Year will help "the gray thing hurry away from me." However, there is also an indirect reference to his desire to push his soul into the sea where the water will wash away all the stains.

In *The Full Moon* O'Sullivan describes a different aspect

of the moon, one that we are not aware of. The moon is described as angry and as it shines over the wasteland the persona feels "fear of her red eye." The moon is normally described as pale, calm, and white. The qualities the poet associates here with the moon are usually connected with the sun. But since he has decided to describe the land of the lost souls, "then even the natural planets have fallen," and therefore changed. Nature has also fallen after Man's fall. The sinner has lost his purity and whiteness of soul and feels desperate. He identifies with the "unhappy dead" and "the drowned" that "stretch up their hands / And toss them to and fro" looking for a helping hand that would pull them out of the deep mire. There is a feeling of abandonment since the sea they are all in is not only deep but also hidden away from sight. The penitent sinner seems to be in a "passionless despair" because he believes that no one will help them. The questions that arise in his mind are whether he can escape the anger of the moon, or whether he can regain the purity he once possessed? At this very moment he is hopeless and unable to change his state.

Mircea Eliade sees the moon as a symbol of death since it disappears from the sky for three days each month, and when it reappears on the fourth day it is reborn. In that light, Eliade considers death a temporary extinction, a necessary withdrawal that leads to rebirth.[13] That is exactly the idea that O'Sullivan wants to convey when he associates the moon with the death of the "lost souls." From the religious point of view, the souls, which have been described as lost, will be eventually reborn. Ultimately they will have an opportunity to start anew, but most importantly, start pure.

In *A Silken Ladder* O'Sullivan dramatizes the sinner's experience in five parts, with a beginning, middle, and end. The choice of "silk," the material the ladder is made of, is significant. A silken ladder is not only so fine and fragile, but also, almost invisible. The symbolism of the ladder is important too, since it is used for ascent as well as descent. Thus the sinner can use it either to ascend to Heaven or descend to Hell and only if he musters enough strength. The poet describes a metaphysical experience that takes place in the sinner's soul and is concretized by the concept of the ladder. O'Sullivan's poem shows the influence of the metaphysical poets on his work since the use of the ladder alludes to George Herbert's "rope of sand" in *The Collar*, and "Jacob's ladder" in Henry Vaughan's *Regeneration*. This is the second poem after *Calvary Hill* that deals with the subject of ascent. The poem takes the reader from the deep wasteland in *The Full Moon* to the ladder with the possibility of moving to a different state.

The experience takes place in a "distant town" during the evening. The faint lights of the little town and the stars in the evening sky are there to show him the "first steps in the drowsy lane." And even though walking in this lane is welcome, the feelings of doubt make him feel a certain amount of uneasiness since "to-morrow shall the morn be gray with rain, / Or sunlight with the fragrant pathway blend." The sinner is presently weary and insecure. O'Sullivan borrowed the idea of the ladder from the Bible to convey his views about man's determination to save his soul. "And he dreamed, and behold a ladder set up on the earth, and the top of it reached to heaven; and behold the angels of God ascending and descending on it" (*Genesis* 28.12).

What theologians call the ladder of contemplation is prefigured in Jacob's dream. The angels use the ladder to ascend toward God and descend to man. According to Saint John of the Cross that ladder has ten steps. The Saint qualified these steps as steps of love, and all the soul has to do is ascend these steps one at a time purifying itself in the process and preparing for the ultimate holy marriage. O'Sullivan was drawn by the way this concept was dealt with by Saint John of the Cross and decided to use it in *A Silken Ladder*.

When the soul/lover starts to ascend the first step it/he is suddenly taken ill, and the cause of illness is the separation of the Bridegroom from his Beloved/Christ, says Saint John of the Cross and adds, "I adjure you, daughters of Jerusalem, if you find my Beloved, tell Him that I am sick with love"

(*Canticles* 5.8). In this stage sickness does not lead to physical death instead, it is the soul that dies "only to sin and to all things that are not God." As the soul proceeds to the second step its health deteriorates. In the meantime, the Bride awaits impatiently the return of her lover. As time goes by and her lover does not appear she decides to get up and go look for Him; "I will rise and seek Him whom my soul loves" (*Canticles* 3.2). Gradually, the soul recovers and gains strength as it ascends to the third step. There the soul is filled with "a burning zeal to work without wearying." At this point, the deeds performed by the soul for the Beloved are evaluated and appear small and almost insignificant. This means the soul has to do more.

When the soul ascends to the fourth step the spirit acquires immeasurable strength that enables it to keep the flesh in total subjection. Furthermore, emphasis is laid on the only aim the soul has which is no other but to achieve a vision of God and union with Him. The powerful desire to be with God pushes the soul upward to the fifth step. Here the soul becomes deeply restless and yearns for the possession of the Beloved. So delay seems to be wearisome and unbearable. As a matter of fact, it is time to "behold the Beloved or die." Arriving to the sixth step the soul is seen anxious to move swiftly in order to meet God and experience His love. The process of purification has been completed and the soul is ready to ascend to the seventh step. It is here that the Bridegroom becomes bold and says, "I thirst for a kiss from these lips" (*Canticles* 1.1).

Boldness leads the soul to the eighth step and there it unites with the Beloved. The soul/lover seizes the Beloved, who is not other than Christ, and is not willing to let Him go. He says, "I found Him whom my heart and soul love; and now that He is mine I will never let Him go" (*Canticles* 3.4). The longing desire of the soul is attained but is it forever? There is a constant and underlying fear that this happy moment can be lost again. On the ninth step the soul burns with "sweet rapture." Obviously the soul has achieved the state of perfection, that is, the state of glory. This is the state in which the soul would continue to exist in bliss because it will burn with the love of God. When the soul ascends to the tenth and last step it is time to be wholly assimilated with God.[14]

In *A Silken Ladder* O'Sullivan speaks of both "rain" and "tears" that fall on "dead hopes," hopes which flew up to heaven but now have dropped "gloomily to earth again." At this point, the poet refers to the separation of the lovers and the slim chance of their reunion. This is the metaphor that suggests the loss of hope the penitent sinner is presently experiencing. The sinner goes on to refer to his soul leaving his body behind so as to embark on his journey to Heaven. In addition, the poet uses images that suggest wetness as he describes the muddy road on which the footprints of the beloved walking away can be detected. The idea that the death of the body occurs before the soul is given a chance to be saved is indirectly conveyed. As the sinner says in the next section of the poem, he has been imprisoned for so long in a lonely and dark cell full of crawling "strange vermin." Thankfully this damp place is filled with a warm light. As the light penetrates his dark cell he becomes aware, for the first time, that life is going on in the small town outside. This is the powerful light of God that strikes and awakens the sinner's soul reminding him of the life he can enjoy in the City of Heaven. He realizes that it is never too late to try to escape from the prison of the dark flesh:

> Methought I was a prisoner lying dead
> In a close room of some grave citadel,
> Where no white gleam did penetrate to tell
> Of day outside and sunny hours that sped;
> But horrid dark was there, and round my head
> Strange vermin crawled: when sudden in the cell
> A warm light broke; the damp walls shook and fell;
> Around my feet the hushed grass carpet spread.

In this poem the reader is reminded that the sinner continues to walk the streets of the city. He comes across a woman who revives in him the nostalgia that "the town was strangely sweet" the moment he looks into her eyes. Naturally, by tracing her footprints he is led to her. Meeting her puts him under a spell and when she leaves and he continues to walk alone in the garden, the feeling of enchantment is stressed. This charm is brought about with the "hot air," and "the smell / Of witching flowers." The incident parallels the one John of the Cross describes which occurs on the eighth step when the Bride and her Lover unite but continue to be afraid of losing each other again.

The life of the sinner clearly changes in the fifth section since now he can see once more the beautiful woman alone in a garden

> ... the hot air
> Hung heavily: enchanted by the smell
> Of witching flowers, you dipped your fair
> And star-abated bosom in their dewy well,
> While the fond lilies kissed your gloomy hair.

In the last section of the poem the reader witnesses a union that occurs only for a few moments, since the sinner refers to "touching hands for a breath in icy fear / Two passing phantoms trembling in the snow." It is evident that everything is so uncertain and that there is so much fear in his heart. He seems to be afraid to feel exultation because that union might never materialize again. The poem ends with the soul on the eighth step. It has to continue the process of cleansing as it ascends the last two steps where the soul finds itself in the land of the ghosts.

The idea of moving from joy to sorrow is compared to man's movement from childhood to adulthood and from innocence to experience, and consequently, to sin. The result is bitterness and gibing which provokes separation. When man sins, his soul is first separated from the Divine, and then, starts to live in a cold deserted land. By the end of the poem the lovers are only "phantoms," and the enchanting warm landscape turns to a deserted land situated in the Frigid Zone. The sinner distinguishes between the beautiful warm landscape his soul experienced momentarily when the hands of the lover and the beloved touched, and the dry cold landscape to which he returns on earth. Only now he can tell what he was missing all the years he wallowed in sin.

The question he poses in the first section is finally answered. It is clear that life gives its place to death, and spring and summer to cold and winter, as joy is replaced by fear. The next day turns out to be "gray with rain," and "the fragrant pathway" vanishes in the land of shadows. It is significant to point out that the "silken ladder" leads the sinner to the land of phantoms. The invisible ladder leads to an invisible land of invisible inhabitants. The abstract situation that O'Sullivan describes in this poem is reflected in the subject matter. But by the same token, the poet succeeds by the selection of the symbolic "silken ladder" to turn this abstract situation into a concrete one. As a result, the sinner is seen in continuous action: he walks, follows his beloved, finds her, loses her, and unites with her at the end in the land of the ghosts. Once the sinner descends to earth he is convinced that he needs to prove himself not only by showing love for others but also helping lost souls. Testing himself will not only purify him further it will also give him the necessary courage to ascend the two remaining steps. The "silken ladder" leads to the land of the *Lonely Women* where the first test takes place.

The Lonely Women is a poem in which O'Sullivan describes the desperate state of the women. And as they wonder if the coming years will bring joy or more sorrow, they remain in a state of apathy. The women are seen twisting and twining "blood-stained wreaths" suggesting the crown of thorns that Christ wore on His head. They do not stop weaving these wreaths even though their fingers are bleeding, a sign that their suffering is continuous and that they seem to have been going through this painful experience for a very long period of time. Moreover, the wreaths that are woven by the women symbolize the circular shape of the trap from which they are unable to break free. Consequently, not only is their pain excruciating but also their endless attempts to break away repeatedly abort. Their despair intensifies, as they become conscious that "around them move the phantoms of the dead." And whenever they look out of the window they seem to be gazing into the void rather than "the crowd" that goes by. They are reminded of the lovers whom they know they will never see again. In a flashback O'Sullivan describes the feast of the dead, that is, the banquet that appeared in the opening poem of the collection. It is at this time that the sinner encounters the desperate women. He realizes that the women represent the lost souls who have dwelled in the Houses of Sin. The feast ceases to be colorful or attractive and becomes macabre and gruesome. O'Sullivan selects all the elements of the *danse macabre* to evoke a vivid image of the reality the soul abides in when living in sin, when pain becomes a way of life, and despair permeates man's whole being. The hopeless women are seen carrying their cross and as they fall under its weight they find themselves amongst the dead since this is the "place of skulls." Moreover, the women never stop tossing "on a grievous bed" because they know that nothing can relieve them of their pain: "no wine-soaked sponge your constant torture lulls." The redeemed persona, who is on the scene, sympathizes with the women who experience "the pain and unheeded sighs, / And marked the grief you struggled to subdue." He has seen the "forgotten tears" in their eyes and felt their deep sorrow and wishes to relieve their pain but is unable of doing so.

In *A Slave of the Street* O'Sullivan deals with the social problem of prostitution. He describes a destitute woman who tries to break free from her bondage, but fails. She happens to be one of the many lonely women he described in the previous poem. As she stands in the "draughty" corner muttering hoarsely "old songs" with a "vague regret" she remembers her past life. But the reader is given an opportunity to peep into some of her ideas such as the way a "coquette" should walk and behave when she detects a customer, or a "sweetheart," approaching her in a drunken state. At dawn she tries to impress her charms on a cab driver whom she asks to take her home on condition that she pays no fee for the trip. The woman is portrayed as desperate and angry and curses continuously, a sign that she is frustrated at having failed to change her miserable life. This is one of the very few poems where O'Sullivan tries to grapple with one of the severe social problems of the nineties.

In *To an Enemy when Dying* the poet portrays the sinner raving on his deathbed. He realizes that it is time to repent as an escape from the bondage of sin. Simultaneously, he is aware that the devil is mocking his efforts and "gloat[ing] upon my last despair." He has been responsible for the change of his soul and the loss of his innocence and purity. The sinner imagines being laid in his grave as "the hungry worms are crawling from the grave" a thought that scares him and motivates him to overcome the evil in his heart. Thus he challenges the devil by saying: "Yea, as you smile, and turn my corpse to fun, / May your lips shrivel when you pass my hearse." This battle that takes place in his soul is a proof of the existence of God. If this voice produced no sound within, then that would mean he was past any help. That would mean no progress, no becoming, no change, and no movement upward. Furthermore, some say that death is annihilation of consciousness; others say that death is the passage of the soul or mind into another dimension of reality. In **Hereafter** Winter says:

> Death is not the end. It is not the end of life, or love, or beauty. It is not the end of anything good, worthwhile, or lovely. It is not the end of those we love, nor is it the end of our own spiritual and moral development. Like sailors looking out over the water, we can only see as far as the horizon that man calls death. But beyond that horizon lies more, so much more, hidden from our eyes, but revealed, item by item, to our minds and our hearts by faith, and through the words of Jesus.

> Evil, not death, is the final enemy of man. Death is the final enemy of man's final enemy. Beyond it lies a new kind of life, where evil has no place at all.[15]

After the poem in which the sinner is seen on his deathbed O'Sullivan writes *A Prayer*. The poem deals with the innumerable lost souls that are praying at night for God's forgiveness. But God does not seem to be listening to their prayers because they have come too late, and so, instead of showing love, He sends wind, fever, and gloom to punish them. The idea that man should not wait till the last moment to ask for God's grace and forgiveness is stressed in this poem. As such there seems to be no hope for them even on Judgment Day when they will get only thunder and lightning as a signal of God's anger. Furthermore, the punishment of the souls will be continuous from seven to seven on a daily basis. The stars will "fall" from heaven and "scourge" the earth, the winter chill will be felt in May, and instead of joy there will be only weeping. Finally, "ghosts," instead of appearing during the night only, will start roaming the earth during the day as well. In the third stanza God is depicted as insensitive and tough since He is not touched with the sighs and tears of the sinners. And the persona questions if it is fair to have to suffer Hell on earth while he is alive and still have to suffer pain upon dying, "A Hell here full of sighing, / And Hell, O God, at dying." And since this happens to be man's lot, then it is better to pray to God to "strike down" with His "great sabre" all "My kindred and my neighbour / The mothers in their labour, / The children in the womb" in order to save them from possible future pain and torture. If the prayers of the sinners are not heard by God then they might as well indulge in lust and pleasure, or seek madness which would absorb them and make them forget their doom. In this poem the persona feels that God is hard on the sinners and tries to speak on their behalf. He complains of God's injustice and sentencing of sinners. Yet God seems adamant in His refusal, He will not accept the late prayers of sinners. And as He persists on punishing the sinners they find it hard to shake off the feeling of despair. They have no alternative but to wish for an escape that will numb their mind making it hard to think.

> Ah drive us from our sadness
> To welcome lust with gladness,
> To rapine and to madness,
> So we forget our doom.

Obviously, in this poem O'Sullivan is referring to the God of the Old Testament who is a severe Judge unwilling to give the sinner a second chance to mend his ways. According to the poet there is always a possibility that the sinner might be turned down, yet the sinner has to take the risk and ask for God's forgiveness or accept the punishment meted out.

In *The Rivals* O'Sullivan deals with death that comes after a long life of sorrow and sin. Normally, when Death appears at the end of man's trip on earth Life finds it very difficult to resist it so it withdraws its protective arms leaving man vulnerable and exposed to death's power. All of a sudden the poet reverses what he has already stated in the first two lines when he makes Death retire and leave Life free to act out its role. "When Death drawn near felt warm the breath of Life / Her arms withdrew; for she was weakened sore." One realizes that the sinner in the last two poems has decided to loosen his grip on life and accept death. Life and Death are portrayed here as rivals vying for the sinner's soul. The latter is described as more powerful suggesting that the possibility of winning the battle is not out of reach. In another context the poet describes Life and Death as two lovers fighting over the sinner's soul. The sinner's soul symbolizes for each one of them the beloved each desires. Gradually, the desire for life becomes overwhelming so much so that Death ends up feeling out of place and withdraws. The poet successfully portrays both Life and Death as rivals who take turns in manipulating the soul of man. It becomes clear to the sinner that both Life and Death have something of value to offer man, but the sinner wants to free himself from Life on earth and this he can do only through

Death. So Death has the potential to offer him life in Heaven something he has yearned for so long. Thus, death becomes attractive since it can lead him to eternal life. Since death can bring eternal life the sinner is finally convinced to accept it.

The soul is led Eastward, and to go Eastward suggests returning to the source of life says John Donne in his poem *Good Friday Riding Westward*,

> Hence is't, that I am carryed towards the West
> This day, when my Soules forme bends towards the East.
> There I should see a Sunne, by rising set,
> And by that setting endlesse day beget.[16]

In *The Voices of the Winds* O'Sullivan depicts a warm wind blowing from the south sea. The sinner wonders if the wind can answer a few questions for him. He decides to ask the wind whether it has seen his beloved. The answer that follows reveals to him that she did go south and that she had "pure white stars in her shining hair." She was seen smiling because she felt free "from grief and strife and all misery." In the second stanza the sinner asks the west wind which way did his love go. The reply he receives informs him that she was seen as a member of a choir of maidens singing sweetly "amongst the brightest she brightest shone / But eyes ere sad, and she seemed alone" and she kneeled and prayed for him. Not receiving the information he requests, and not having found his beloved, the sinner insists on repeating his question. This time the answer is from the east wind that claims to have seen her amongst "spectres shudder[ing] in frenzied fear / 'Mid those phantom forms thy love in the frost" was wringing her hands and weeping because she feels lost and yearns to be free as the wind. Finally, the sinner asks the wild north wind to lead him to his love and this time the wind accepts to guide him. He is led through the "cheerless churchyard" and "crushing tomb" where his love stands knowing that "when life is sped, / With its flame and fever, all hope is dead." When the sinner, at last, sees the Beloved he realizes that his soul is not yet ready for the new state and so does not unite with her. He also realizes that once the soul leaves the body then there is no way it can ever return to it.

In this poem O'Sullivan uses the wind as the central symbol. At the beginning it is heard sighing softly, then it becomes restless, and before too long it begins to howl. The wind implies the changes the sinner's feelings go through. At the beginning, the sinner believes he can find his beloved but, as time goes by, he loses all hope that he will ever unite with her. The poem starts with a warm wind but ends with a cold one. The wind is the only natural force that is free to travel the universe. Moreover, the wind is seen in action as it changes the state of the sea from "restless" to "sobbing." Shifting to the human soul O'Sullivan suggests that the soul is happy and carefree when pure. But as it begins to lose its innocence by indulging in sin, it encounters loss and despair, and finally, pain as it faces its moment of death. So from smiles and songs it moves to sighs, shrieks, and howls. The wind and the sea represent the male and female, the spirit and the flesh undergoing a metaphysical experience. The wind and the sea are seen interacting and sensing each other's presence. The wind and the sea complement each other in the universe. The wind is felt but cannot be seen and so remains abstract, while the sea can be seen, and therefore, is concrete. Both parallel the invisible spirit and the visible body. Furthermore, after the body immerses in the sea the soul is carried off by the wind to heaven. When O'Sullivan wrote his poetry he was certainly aware of the symbolic significance of both the wind and the sea. Watts argued that the Holy Spirit is manifested in the wind and fire. The wind is regarded as "masculine in its strength and feminine in its softness, and fire is masculine in its brilliance and feminine in its warmth and volatility." In addition, water is associated with the spirit since it is considered an agent through which it works for "unless a man is born of water and the Spirit, he cannot enter into the kingdom of heaven" (*John* 3.5). The Holy Spirit is the breath of God's life, the flame of His glory, and the stream of His love.[17]

"Except ye convert and become as little children, ye shall not enter into the kingdom of heaven," (*Matthew* 18. 3). The soul of the child is not yet corrupted by the ways of the world or dulled by the lethargy of custom. Therefore the child is capable of looking on the creation as God intended all men to look upon it as a wonderful and glorious thing and as the garment of God. The renovation of the soul can be achieved by the Spirit and the grace of God (*Titus* 3.5). "For we ourselves were once foolish, disobedient, led astray, slaves to various passions and pleasures, passing our days in malice and envy" (*Titus* 4.4). And only when the goodness and the loving kindness of God and the Savior appear in man's life will he be saved. "Saved not because of deeds done by us in righteousness, but in virtue of His own mercy, by the washing of regeneration and renewal in the Holy Spirit which He poured out upon us richly through Jesus Christ" (*Titus* 4.5). As such man can hope to gain eternal life.

In *God's Hour* O'Sullivan describes a purely metaphysical experience as the soul ascends to the tenth step of the ladder and the desired union with the Divine takes place. One senses echoes of George Herbert's poem *The Collar* as the penitent sinner puts his soul in the hands of God. As he lies in his bed expecting the end he sees "the spirit of God," hears the sweet songs of Heaven, and smells the odor of flowers. He is thankful that he has been given this opportunity to experience this wonderful feeling even though he is a "poor clod." He immediately begins conversing with God. After a little while God bends down and looks into his eyes and tells him that He desires to have him. And so God extends His hand, He grasps the penitent's hand, and pulls him upward. At the moment this happens the remains of any impurities fall off. And when God tells the penitent that He wants him for His own he sees all the angels bowing down and looking at him. He feels God's breath on him that further purifies him and relieves him from any pain he has suffered on earth. At last the penitent's soul is reborn. In this poem the poet describes the kindness of God as opposed to what he said in *A Prayer*. Here

God is seen forgiving and loving to the sinful soul. But that is because the sinner repented on time and did enough penance to warrant God's love and forgiveness. In this poem the soul is seen entering Heaven and beginning its new life in the court of God amidst the angels. The ascent to Calvary has paid off. The sinner's soul has succeeded in becoming as free as the wind by breaking the fetters that held it in earthly bondage. In the previous poem the penitent sinner was seen burying the body "in the cheerless churchyard." Once the soul is set free then it can travel with the wind to Heaven.

Saint Augustine says: "my soul is all in ruins; do thou repair it. There are things in it that must offend thy gaze, I confess and know, but who shall cleanse it? Or to what other besides thee shall I cry out from my secret sins Cleanse me O Lord?" When the purgation of man's soul has been completed and "the Bridegroom has bestowed his ring and kiss upon the bride then the marriage is consummated."[18] When Jesus explained to Nicodemus what it means to be reborn, he said: "Marvel not that I said unto thee, Ye must be born again. The wind bloweth where it listeth, and thou hearest the sound thereof, but canst not tell whence it cometh, and whither it goeth; so is every one that is born of the spirit" (*John* 3. 7-8). The life the soul experiences after the union with God is known as the Spiritual Marriage. In this new life, metaphorically, God and the soul are united. This entails a complete annihilation of the self. The self is wholly absorbed into the Divine so that no difference in essence exists any longer between it and God. This is the process that completes the spiritualization of man. In this manner man's new life begins on the spiritual level, a life very different from the physical one he led on earth.

For the End is a poem that rounds off the experience O'Sullivan has described throughout this volume. It suggests the end of a lifetime's effort to achieve union with the Divine, and the end of life on earth. It is an inevitable state, something to look forward to, for "it is unto man when he is sad / Pleasant to think that he shall surely die." The end is not a state to lament because through death man can acquire the kingdom of

Heaven. The pain around him leads his thoughts "to dwell upon the coolness of the grave." The poet describes the "fevered earth" in contrast to the "coolness of the grave." The sorrow and pain he feels presently contrast with the joy and the pleasure he will experience in the future. This poem puts an end to the journey the penitent sinner undertook to the Houses of Sin. He learns that all these houses offer many pleasures but they are all linked to pain and sorrow. After all, these pleasures prove futile because ultimately man is bound to end in the grave. This is the same idea referred to at the end of **Poems** where everything related to the physical world turns to "ashes" and "dust." All these pleasures destroy the purity of the soul and are responsible for torturing it with fear. It is wise to admit the futility of these pleasures and try to find the "silken ladder" to climb up to Heaven. This poem takes the reader back to the first poem *Remnants* where the idea of futility is conveyed. Consequently, the living soul is forced to go through the kingdom of death where "there is no moon in the black place and all the devils or ghouls of Hell are loose, threatening, and only the dim flames of smoldering corpses are to illuminate our weary wandering."[19]

This volume is an allegorical account of the mysterious workings of grace. The reader watches the sinner/pilgrim enter into a state of interior illumination where he is prepared to apprehend the presence of God and hear His voice. The spiritual part of man, is eventually reborn, made bright and quick as light while the fleshly part remains dull, heavy, and bound to the earth. In actuality when sin and corruption gain entrance into the human soul, then it becomes "an habituation of darkness and death," and as the Lord stands outside and knocks, the soul surfeited and sleepy "shuts his door, and leaves God out all night."

> Many a time hast thou knockt, and I have shut
> the doors against thee, thou hast often called,
> and I would not answer, sleeping and waking,
> early and late, day and night have I refused

> instruction, and would not be healed. And now, O
> my God, after all this rebellion and uncleanness,
> thou come and lodge with me.[20]

O'Sullivan's redeemed persona has learned through his quest that turning to Christ for help and admitting Him into his soul was the only way to redemption and so he teaches the sinner to open his heart to Christ's call. When the human spirit is ready, God enters it without hesitation or waiting. It is written in *Revelations* that the Lord told the people: "Behold I stand at the door and knock and wait. If any man let me in, I will sup with him. You need not look either here or there. He is no farther away than the door of thy heart."[21]

"He that followeth Me, walketh not in darkness saith the Lord" (*John* 8. 12). By these words Christ instructed man how he ought to imitate His life and manners if he is to be truly enlightened and delivered from all the blindness and "vanity of vanities" in his heart (*Ecclesiastes* 1. 2). What has to dominate man's heart is love for God and a willingness to serve Him only. Vanity is to seek after perishing riches and to trust in them. It is vanity to follow the desires of the flesh and to labor for what he must afterward suffer grievous punishment. It is also vanity to mind only this present life and to fail to foresee those things that are to come. It is vanity to set his life on whatever speedily passes away and not to hasten forward where everlasting joy abides. Man must endeavor, therefore, to withdraw his heart from the love of visible material things and turn himself to the spiritual. For whoever follows his sensuality stains his conscience and loses the favor of God. Finally, O'Sullivan stresses the idea that the Houses of Sin are not worth living in for long even though going through them can be beneficial. Experiencing temptation instead of resisting it can lead to a more fulfilling and complete salvation. Learning about the demon that resides in man's soul is more advantageous than suppressing it or avoiding it because it leads to a better understanding of his self. Learning to challenge his demon and fight it consciously is a test of strength. After all, accepting the weaknesses that characterize our humanity is the essence of wisdom. To negate evil is to allow evil to persist. Obviously evil in Paradise was accepted and assimilated. That is why Adam and Eve had to taste the forbidden fruit and acquire the knowledge of evil for themselves and for mankind. In this light the disobedience of man becomes a necessary and painful experience that had to be lived. Without the fall of man evil would have continued to persist because Christ would not have come to earth to vanquish the devil and, therefore, would not have taught man the way to defeat evil.

It is essential that the soul overcomes the desire for worldly things, strives upward with faith, and receives the grace meted out by God in order to be lifted up. In the traditional language of Catholic mysticism there are three steps: purgation, illumination, and perfection that man should follow. The active way is the effort of the will to free the soul from sensual distractions. This action fulfills the first two steps that are purgation and illumination. Furthermore, the active way with the ordinary help of grace, purges the sense and the spirit and culminates in an assent of the will to faith that is known as illumination. As for the passive way where there is more abundant grace than before there is a cessation of activity on behalf of the soul so that the sense and the spirit may be purged by God. Once the approval to proceed toward the union with the Divine is granted, then there is no other state than that of perfection that prevails. The soul cannot achieve its final goal by its own labor no matter how vigorously it labors to prepare itself for God. Emptying itself of desire is not enough. It needs God's grace to purify it completely and prepare it for the Holy marriage. In ***The Dark Night of the Soul*** John of the Cross says:

> It befits the soul, however, to contrive to labour, in so far as it can, on its own account, to the end that it may purge and perfect itself, and thus may merit being taken by God into that Divine care wherein it becomes healed of all things that it was unable of itself to cure. Because, however

greatly the soul itself labours, it cannot actively purify itself so as to be in the least degree prepared for the Divine union of perfection of love, if God takes not its hand and purges it not in that dark fire.[22]

But to arouse oneself from the bower of sensuality, to free oneself from the siren song of the worldly choir so as to hear the knock and the call of Christ and open the door, now stiff with rust, is not the work of a moment. Only Christ can give light and strength to the penitent to find and walk in the new way. It is a long dreary journey and it has many steps. Thomas Vaughan warns man of the brevity of life and reminds him that he has to be ready if he wants to unite with God. He says: "Thou must prepare thyself till thou art comfortable to Him whom thou wouldst entertain, and that in every respect."[23] Saint John implies the same idea when he says:

Christ will come unto thee, and show thee His consolations, if thou prepare for Him worthy mansion within thee...O faithful soul, make ready thy heart for this Bridegroom, that he may vouchsafe to come unto thee, and dwell within thee, For thus saith He: if any love Me, he will keep My words, and we will come unto him, and will make our abode with him (*John* 14. 25).

According to Berdayeav the end comes "only through a bond between the human spirit and the spirit of God." He proceeded to clarify this statement claiming that "Spiritual liberation is always a turning to a profounder depth than the spiritual principle in man, it is a turning to God." Therefore, the spiritual liberation of man is the realization of personality in man. It is the attainment of wholeness, and at the same time, it is unwearied conflict.[24] In **The Houses of Sin** O'Sullivan has proven that it is possible for man to liberate himself from sin, and he has shown the way that leads to the union with the Divine. The journey and the ascent to Heaven and final residence in the embrace of God can be attained by every individual soul even though the road is full of thorns and obstacles. As a matter of fact, O'Sullivan believed that the journey could prove to be the only way out of the web of the *fin-de-siècle*, or maybe could prove an acceptable solution to the dilemmas that preoccupied many at that time.

Chapter three concludes with the realization of the ultimate goal that is the union of the soul with the Divine. This volume ends with a reward, a spiritual satisfaction for having achieved what he set out to obtain. The soul ascends all ten steps of the ladder and finds God's embrace ready to receive him. The marriage is consummated and the soul is in ecstasy. From this moment on the soul will experience only bliss in its eternal abode.

NOTES
Chapter III

[1] Vincent O'Sullivan, *Houses of Sin* (London: Smithers, 1897). All citations are to this edition.

[2] Thomas à Kempis, *Of the Imitation of Christ: Four Books* (Oxford: Oxford University Press, 1940) 34-36.

[3] A Kempis, 67.

[4] Merritt Y. Hughes, ed., *John Milton: Complete Poems and Prose* (Indianapolis: The Odessey Press, 1957).

[5] R.W. Stott, *Basic Christianity* (London: Inter-Varsity, 1973) 65.

[6] James Finley, *Merton's Palace of Nowhere: A Search for God Through Awareness of the True Self* (Notre Dame: Ave Maria Press, 1978) 65.

[7] Paul Tournier, *The Person Reborn* (London: SCM Heinemann, 1966) 151.

[8] Nikolai Berdyaev, *Slavery and Freedom* (New York: Charles Scribner, 1964) 234-235.

[9] Michel Quoist, *Christ is Alive* (Dublin: Gill & Macmillan, 1971) 67.

[10] Quoist 13.

[11] Quoist 104.

[12] Quoist, 98.

[13] Mircea Eliade, *Images and Symbols: Studies in Religious Symbolism* (New York: Sheed & Ward, 1969) 166.

[14] Tournier, *The Person Reborn* 169.

[15] David Winter, **Hereafter: What Happens after Death** (Illinois: Harold Shaw Publishers, 1977) 91.

[16] Herbert J. C. Grierson, **The Poems of John Donne** (Oxford: Oxford University Press, 1966) 336-337.

[17] Alan Watts, **Behold the Spirit** (New York: Vintage Books, 1971) 173.

[18] Stott, **Basic Christianity** 75.

[19] Heinrich Zimmer, and Joseph Campbell, eds., **The King and the Corpse: Tales of the Soul's Conquest of Evil** (New Jersey: Princeton University Press, 1937) 222.

[20] John of the Cross, **The Dark Night of the Soul**, trans. Kurt F. Reinhardt (New York: Frederich Ungar Publishing Co., 1957) 75.

[21] A Kempis, **Of the Imitation of Christ** 13-14.

[22] John of the Cross, **The Dark Night of the Soul** 337-338.

[23] Alan Rudrun ed., **The Works of Thomas Vaughan** (Oxford: Clarendon Press, 1984) 187.

[24] Berdyaev, **Slavery and Freedom** 246.

Chapter IV
The Soul in Bliss

Dissatisfaction with the contemporary world, restlessness, anxiety, and moral malaise were of course the after effects that resulted from the historical situation as well as the loosening of the social framework and the collapse of religious belief. The *fin-de-siècle* implied a morbid spirit beleaguered by fluctuations of mood. This general uneasiness was often reflected in the writings of the time. As Nordeau noted, it was the time when "degenerates must succumb. They can neither adapt themselves to the conditions of nature and civilization, nor maintain themselves in the struggle for existence against the healthy."[1] But Arthur Symons sought for a vantage that would allow full aesthetic appreciation of this sort of literature without moral judgment or social commitment. Simultaneously, as the faculty of reason began to lose its role as a dependable guide, imagination and feeling were there to replace it. The men of the nineties were known to give themselves up to their dreams and their passions and in their writings they saw fit to cultivate now one now another of the feelings which they deeply cherished. Furthermore, by clinging to feelings as the only reliable thing ennobled their souls and encouraged them to rise above their distress and doubts. Nordeau states that

> ...the *fin-de-siècle* mood is the impotent despair of a sick man who feels himself dying by inches in the midst of an eternally living nature blooming insolently forever. It means the end of an established order, which for thousands of years has satisfied logic, fettered depravity, and in every art matured something of beauty.[2]

One can safely assume unreservedly that the Decadent soul was not passive; on the contrary, it was hyperactive, since it strove passionately for its liberation from the bondage of the material world. To achieve that state meant they had to free themselves from the horror of reality by means of retiring into the sanctuary of their feelings or their imagination.

So it may be that this movement, which accepted

as a badge the reproach of decadence, is the first hot flush of the only ascendant movement of our times; and that the strange and bizarre artists who lived tragic lives and made tragic end of their lives, are the mad priests of that new romanticism whose aim was the transmutation of vision into personal power.[3]

But to Nordeau there was a lot more to Decadence. He argued that "besides moral insanity and emotionalism, there is to be observed in the degenerate a condition of elemental weakness and despondency, which according to the circumstances of his life assumes the form of pessimism."[4]

Vincent O'Sullivan, like his contemporaries, trusted the "inner world" immensely because it was the only place where he could discover his buried soul. But finding his soul was only the first step since what mattered most was to attempt to carry it up to Heaven in the same way as his persona has done so successfully. Some of the agonizing tragic utterances of the Decadents could be suppressed only by turning to religion for help and consolation. To some of the hopeless men of the nineties God became the only reality. They believed that whoever sought and discovered the Divine would find repose, lasting happiness, and even refuge from the chaotic world that tormented him.

The chief characteristics of the decadence were perversity, artificiality, egotism and curiosity and these characteristics are not all inconsistent with a sincere desire to find the last fine shade, the quintessence of things; to fix it fleetingly; to be a disembodied voice, and yet the voice of a human soul.[5]

In the two previous chapters the reader witnessed O'Sullivan tracing the passage of the soul from the earth to the grave and beyond in its effort to achieve total freedom. The hardships the soul encounters in this passage freed the soul, from its earthly fetters, and from the abyss of Hell. Like the persona of ***Poems*** the poet hoped that after the agonizing quest he, too, would attain a state of joy by experiencing the mystical state of marriage with the Divine. O'Sullivan's view of the quest does not differ dramatically from that of Mircea Eliade who stated that "the center of the world is at the heart of reality." As for man he could by "a short cut and in a natural manner transcend the human condition, and recover the Divine condition as a Christian would say, the condition before the fall."[6] O'Sullivan also believed fervently that man could recover the Divine condition he enjoyed before the fall. According to Ann Belford Ulanov man longs "to return to a symbiotic unity with God, to be safely held within the greatest possible power of being." Man, she argues, "yearns for security and dependency, entirely supported by God's love." Man also seeks "containment within a mystery that will enfold [his] transiency within eternity." After all, man "wants to be grounded in Being, just as a child is joined to its Mother's Being." Therefore "any move toward independence, any move away from symbiotic unity, is imbued with sadness. To be oneself is to be desolate, to be ejected from life's center." By "transcending the created world" of matter, man is able to achieve eternity in the court of Heaven. Clearly, that is a better life than life on earth, which is characterized as the source of intense torture.[7] As a result the world of Heaven becomes the Ultimate Reality man seeks. A world that radiates with truth, a world that each man can attain through repentance and the actual defeat of matter. Finally, in order to achieve the Golden Jerusalem man has to go through death and the abyss of Hell for without death there can be no life. Therefore before emerging one has first to submerge into the vast sea. The quest is deemed necessary because according to Christian mysticism man is separated from God by an abyss. So even though man may want to return to God, he cannot if God does not decide to have him. Consequently, it is not enough for man to exert the effort God has to respond to his prayers and infuse his soul with grace. Only then can man's soul be illumined and elevated, and only then can he set off on his quest and ascend the ladder that will take him out of the abyss and lead him to God's embrace. In ***The Dark Night of the Soul*** John of the Cross envisions the Divine before uniting with it and presents the process of ascent step by step. Saint John of the Cross describes the sinner in complete darkness, but with an inner light brightly alight, that ultimately helps him discover the ladder he will soon begin to climb.

1

In a dark night!
My longing heart aglow with love,
Oh, blessed lot!
I went forth unseen
From my house that was at last in deepest rest.

2

Secure and protected by darkness!
I climbed the secret ladder, in disguise,
Oh, blessed lot!
In darkness, veiled and concealed I went
Leaving behind my house in deepest rest.

3

Oh, blissful night!
Oh, secret night, when I remained unseeing and
    unseen,
Where the flame burning in my heart
Was my only light and guide.

4

This inward light,
A safer guide than noonday's brightness,
Showed me the place where He awaited me,
My soul's Beloved,
A place of solitude.

5

Oh, night that guided me!

Oh, night more lovely than the rosy dawn!
Oh, night whose darkness guided me
To that sweet union,
In which the lover and Beloved are made one.

6

Upon the flower of my breast,
Kept undefiled for Him alone,
He fell asleep,
While I was waking,
Caressing Him with gentle cedars' breeze.

7

And when Aurora's breath
Began to spread His curled hair,
His gentle hand
He placed upon my neck,
And all my senses were in bliss suspended.
Forgetful of myself,
My head reclined on my Beloved,
The world was gone
And all my cares at rest,
Forgotten all my grief among the lilies.

Saint Teresa conveys a similar idea when she says:

When a soul unto its God
Submits indeed
And from every worldly thing
Is wholly freed,
To it as a tree of life
The Cross is given
And a path delectable
That leads to Heaven.[8]

In O'Sullivan's two volumes the persona, and indirectly the poet, is seen using the ladder to achieve the union with the Divine. Thus the persona's journey suggests "the internal circuitous quest [that] follows the lover's union with his female contrary, symbolized in an apocalyptic marriage like that in *Revelations*."[9] In the process of the quest the persona is seen not only climbing upward but also moving, simultaneously, inward until he reaches the deepest regions of his soul. All along there is a deep wish to achieve the desired world of Heaven as well as a strong impulse to escape the hardships of life either by suicide or death. "Let us be glad and rejoice, and give honor to him, for the marriage of the Lamb is come, and his wife hath made herself ready" (*Revalations*. 19.7-8). The marriage of the soul with the Divine does take place at the end of **The Houses of Sin** and that is certainly something to rejoice about. The landscape changes completely as the redeemed soul is bathed in the bright light of God.

Unlike the Romantic hero who quests for a macabre union with his female emanation in death, or who creates epipsyches that symbolize the antithesis of life and death, or yet who searches for demonic lovers, O'Sullivan's persona quests simply for the union with the Divine. O'Sullivan borrowed the specific romantic convention and used it to create concretely the image of the soul as the Beloved. In addition, he creates the metaphor of the marriage of the two lovers to represent the union between the persona's soul and the Divine. This does not mean that the element of the macabre or that the antithesis between life and death are overlooked. After all, "Long and perilous are the paths by which the lover seeks his Beloved. They are peopled by caves, sighs, and tears," but they are also "lit up with love." And even though his quest includes death it is to be interpreted within the religious context he has provided. Death becomes the most effective means of annihilating the body and freeing the soul for its journey to Heaven. Moreover, the persona/lover is not a romantic demonic lover but, a sinner who has wounded the Lord and who decides to repent if he is to achieve salvation.

O'Sullivan also used the theme of death because it is capable of bringing man to the grave, to the earth, to nature. It is that union with the earth that will give man the opportunity to enjoy a better life on a spiritual eternal plane. The redeemed soul of **Poems** returns in **The Houses of Sin** to lead one of the many lost souls from the abyss to eternal joy. It is known that the soul, the Divine part of man, is that immortal aspect of him that yearns for freedom from the body that chains it to earth. Death the persona realizes is a *bona fide* method that can dissolve the bondage, and set the soul free to travel unobstructed toward its final destination where it can achieve its desired union. According to Heinrich Zimmer "nothing dies, nothing perishes, nothing suffers annihilation utterly. Neither virtue, nor energy is lost. Destruction, death is but an outer mask of transformation into something better or something worse, higher or lower."[10] Therefore, ritualistically as well as religiously, death proves it is the only means that has the potential to transform the soul and raise it up to Heaven.

As has been already mentioned in the first chapter, the woman or the mother is symbolic of the Holy Virgin or a Saint who is willing to guide the persona on its route to Heaven. The earth or the grave from which life emerges and to which it returns is necessary, hence the statement of dust to dust. The woman portrayed in O'Sullivan's poetry is not symbolic of chaos and death, as such, she is not a death-giving mother but a life-giving one. Subsequently, her embrace is not deathly, nor is her womb a tomb. As a result, she is not feared or avoided but desired. The woman is easily identified with the sea into which the persona wants to submerge, or the grave into which he wants to be buried. Both the sea and the grave are images used extensively by O'Sullivan. It is noteworthy that both these images are associated with the woman who often appears as a beloved and as a mother, and rarely as a temptress.

For O'Sullivan the lover is symbolic of the body and the beloved of the soul. In many of the poems the reader sees the persona in situations where he attempts to unite with a woman. The poet transforms this act into a metaphor for the lover/beloved or the body/soul. But unlike the Victorian poets, he did not think that the union of the opposites was all man had to achieve. The union of the opposites is necessary only for the acquisition of psychological wholeness, but man still has to give up the body if he wants to transcend. Therefore desire for the union is essential since it brings about completion of Being on the psychological level. On the religious level, the soul has to transcend in order to join the Divine. The latter requires a physical separation of the body from the soul. Therefore, the persona is seen attaining a psychological completion because without it he cannot hope for transcendence. Failure to do so will impede him to fulfill the only goal he has in life, which is the union with the Divine. God is knowledge, God is love, God is power, and if man succeeds in uniting with God then man attains ultimate knowledge, enjoys pure love, and holds full power over his self, and the world. The union with the Divine suggests the superiority of the spirit and its ability to subdue matter.

O'Sullivan believed that the infinite impinged on the finite and in a sense infiltrated it. For O'Sullivan to fulfill his goal, that of the union with the Divine, man has to exert an effort in finding a way to dispose of the body as soon as possible because he is aware that it hampers his soul from ascending to Heaven's court. The material has got to be overcome, and the finite left behind, for they prove the major obstacles with which man has to grapple. Evidently, man has to look within in order to find what he needs to start and complete his spiritual quest. In other words, holding fast to one's center seems to be necessary if man is to succeed. That brings to mind Robert Browning's lines in which he says:

> Truth is within ourselves; it takes no rise
> From outward things, whate'er you may believe,
> There is an inmost center in us all,
> Where truth abides in fulness, and around,
> Wall upon wall, the gross flesh hems it in,
> This perfect, clear perception which is truth.
> A buffling and perverting carnal mesh
> Binds it, and makes all error, and to know
> Rather consists in opening out a way

> Whence the imprisoned splendour may escape,
> Than in effecting entry for a light
> Supposed to be without.[11]

Moreover, O'Sullivan believed that God dwells in every human soul. He dwells there as He dwells in a temple because there His sovereignty is recognized, adored, praised, and asked for help. And finally, it is from there that he dispenses His favors.

In a number of poems O'Sullivan creates images by which he identifies the spirit with the Divine, with goodness, and with the male; and nature with the material, with the fearful, and with the sexual female. So sometimes the female is depicted as a temptress whose wiles the male cannot, and does not, want to resist. But the temptress is closely associated with death, which proves a desirable state. On other occasions, O'Sullivan creates the image of the male and equates it to the body of man and sexuality, while the image of the female he associates with the soul that tries to free itself from male domination that is, from the body. To succeed man needs to have faith in Christ and the Holy Passion. O'Sullivan reverses the Jungian concept of male/spirit and female/body to suit his religious ideas. Not only does he project the lover /body as the male principle that hampers the soul, he also links the soul/beloved that quests for the divine union with the female principle. O'Sullivan continues to develop his ideas when he draws a distinction between the soul and the spirit. The former, states the poet, is man's valuable possession, while the latter is the instrument the Divine uses to reach man, to inspire him, and to cleanse his soul. O'Sullivan represents the spirit as the wind: it is the image he uses to convey the concept of the Holy Ghost. O'Sullivan's distinctions between body and soul as well as between soul and spirit spring originally from the following verse. "And the very God of peace sanctify you wholly; and I pray God your whole spirit and soul and body be preserved blameless unto the coming of our Lord Jesus Christ." (*I Thessalonians* 5,23). The two volumes of poetry form an extended allegorical account of the mysterious manner by which grace works. In both, the poet follows the persona/pilgrim until he achieves a state of interior illumination that prepares him to apprehend the Image of God and to hear His voice. Finally, the persona's soul joins other redeemed souls in God's court. And, all together they "flow to the goodness of the Lord, for wheat, and for wine, and for oil, and for the young of the flock and of the herd; and their soul shall be as a watered garden; and they shall not sorrow any more at all" (*Jeremiah* 30.12).

There are two worlds in O'Sullivan's poetry: the one is the visible world of appearances that is full of deceit, evil, materialism, ignorance, and ugliness and is responsible in driving man to dejection and sorrow. The other is the invisible world that is ideal and beautiful because it is the world of Heaven where ultimate Truth exists, and in which man attains his immortality in the face of God. The former is extensively described in both volumes and corresponds to the abyss, and the latter, is presented at the end of **Poems** and is no other but the court of Heaven. O'Sullivan suggests through his poetry that God is the most obvious Being in the world. He is absolutely self-evident, the simplest, clearest, and closest reality of life and consciousness. Nothing is more real or more concrete, more actual, or more present. Man remains unaware of God because his vision is blurred by sin. But God and the union with Him are the two most significant realities that lie in the depth of the human soul. All man needs to do is search for these realities since finding them will definitely free him and eventually feel happiness. Joseph C. Pearce says that

> Reality is not a fixed entity. It is a contingent interlocking of moving events. And events do not just happen to us. We are an integral part of every event. We enter in the shape of events, even as we long for an absolute in which to rest. It may be just this longing for an absolute in which our concepts might not have to be responsible for our percepts, and so indirectly

our reality, that explains the hostility of our ordinary intellect to these shadowy modes of mind.[12]

As has been already mentioned, O'Sullivan also hearkened to Saint Augustine's words and, makes his persona turn inward to find the Image of God. After enlightenment takes place the soul can grasp the "Vestiges" of God in nature before it turns inward to look for His Image. At the beginning, he may not find it because the sin of our first parents defaced it and even though the sacrifice of Christ restored it, still his sins make it hard to see. Yet it is man's responsibility to look for God's image and revive it with the help of His grace. It must be remembered that this is not an act that can be easily accomplished without undertaking a mystical journey. This is where the difference between the active and the passive way lies. Generally man tends toward a state of inactivity, yet he is forced to blend with events which help him experience the active state. In O'Sullivan's poetry action clarifies the sinner's vision. It is action that leads the soul to discover the inner reality that is no other than God's presence. As for the passive way it is compared to sickness that leads nowhere. In fact, passivity prolongs the fallen state and the soul continues to wallow in sin.

The inner reality is beaming with light but the sinful man who has become a creature of darkness cannot see it. O'Sullivan's persona proves that man is weak and foolish and requires constant guidance. Only Christ, the Virgin Mary, or a Saint can guide him. Turning to them and praying for the Divine light of the Holy Ghost is the only feasible means of acquiring the necessary aid to see the radiance of God that exists in his soul. In this context, James Finley says that the closer man draws to "the roots of [his] existence, to the naked being of [his] self," he finds himself at a point "in ontological communion" with God. This process helps him discover "an awareness of [his] existence for [he] discover[s] a new vantage point from which [he] gaze[s] out at the world as if for the first time."[13]

Thomas à Kempis expressed a similar view when he spoke of man being united within himself when he said that man "becometh inwardly simple and pure, so much the more and higher things doth he understand without labour; for that he receiveth intellectual light from above."[14] Undoubtedly, the stress lies on knowing one's self since it is both the hindrance and the path that leads to God. And à Kempis also asks "who hinders and troubles thee more than the unmortified affections of thine own heart? An humble knowledge of thyself is a surer way to God than a deep search after learning."[15] Coming to know oneself brings harmony and a union between the body and soul. That union is essential because it makes man realize first the futility of the body, then shun it, and therefore, step toward the union with the Divine. No man can rise beyond the physical before he attains harmony on a psychological level.

According to Heinrich Zimmer, "the archetype of all weddings is the union of heaven and earth, and the hero must learn that completeness consists in opposites coexisting through conflict, and that the harmony he aspires for is a resolution of irreducible tensions." He must come to grips with the forces of evil and for that he needs to follow the hidden road of "the dolorous quest." Hence his quest becomes "an allegory of the agony of self-completion through the mastery and assimilation of conflicting opposites."[16] As the senses are mortified, the passions silenced, and the desires appeased and put to sleep, the soul goes forth on its journey in search of the Divine. This is the same process that Saint John of the Cross, calls the way of illumination. While the soul is on the road God nourishes and refreshes it, but more often than not while it receives nourishment and refreshment it lies in apathy. This stage takes place during the first night of the quest. And since going through the first night is not enough the soul has to continue its journey for one more night in order to attain the union with God. The quest helps the soul go from self-love and affection of material objects to inflicting death on itself in order to attain the blissful life in God. For O'Sullivan the reconciliation of opposites was a mystical experience in which man is seen finding the psychological self, which he eventually gives up, because it is temporal, in order to achieve the eternal union with the Divine. In his poetry, the poet succeeds in fusing the ascent to the Divine by harrowing Hell with the psychological experience of the unconscious. O'Sullivan intended his poetry to be experienced because he considered it mystical, overwhelming, emotional, and personal, and not understood or justified through factual evidence. After all, by following the mystic path he ended up creating works that reflected the mystic way with its various aspects such as the temperamental, the individual, and ultimately, the visionary.

According to Joan Ferrente "the integration of Self, the completion of man through union with woman," is both a secular as well as a religious ideal that Dante dealt with.[17] This desired integration is possible only in Heaven, or in a vision, and only when the woman is dead. O'Sullivan refers to the dead beloved on countless occasions. The image most of the times refers to the death of the persona's soul, with the exception of *Wheat and Clover* where a resurrection occurs. Nonetheless, Ferrente believes that man can achieve this integration not by rejecting woman's love, but by affirming and transforming it. In this light, the persona by accepting temptations he tries to transform them to his advantage. It is evident that this Dantesque achievement appealed immensely to O'Sullivan.

Harold Bloom claims that "psychologically the patterns of the apocalypse of the imagination stem from the child's vision of a more titanic universe that the English Romantics were so reluctant to abandon."[18] O'Sullivan's child is no different. The purity of the child's soul and its vision help the adult find out about the state of his own soul before sin set in. Furthermore, Bloom says that "the Romantic Movement is from nature to the imagination's freedom and the imagination's freedom is frequently purgatorial; redemptive in directive but destructive of the social self. The quest is to widen consciousness as well as to intensify it, and of course to find paradise means self-consciousness."[19] In O'Sullivan the movement is from the physical, from the false self, and from

Hell to Purgatory, in an attempt to cleanse the soul and prepare it for the holy marriage in Heaven. Furthermore, man's quest widens and intensifies his religious consciousness since achieving knowledge of the psychological self is not enough. For O'Sullivan consciousness acquires a metaphysical meaning and as such is crucial to man's redemption.

Man is encountered relentlessly by the polarities and interplay of life and death, sky and earth, night and day, male and female, past and future, by what is within and that which is not. He is confounded not only by the irreducible two but by still further complexities in seemingly infinite variations. Thus there is no alternative save to come to terms with the world's wide range of tensions, as with its conjunctions of opposites, to learn to choose and discriminate. The outer senses present the images to the senses so that both God and the devil are projected in even greater beauty. Beneath these images, God targets the soul in order to teach it wisdom while the devil aims to deceive. To achieve his objective the devil presents images in the guise of good, an illustration of that appears in O'Sullivan's poem *The Triumph*.

In both **Poems** and **The Houses of Sin** love in life is frustrated because it is directed toward the physical, whereas death offers a promise of consummation and fulfillment. Hence once the body disappears, the soul begins to love freely because the individual attains his true identity or ideal selfhood in death. According to Wallace Fowlie "love is always search, aspiration, impulse. It is always dominated by the supreme exigency of unity. It is the voyage with no homecoming, the loss of self. Love can never be dissociated from its sacerdotal significance and its mystical origin."[20]

Disappointed with their age, the artists of the *fin-de-siècle* experimented with manners, morals, and modes of expression, which were considered outrageous by the majority of the people. In other words, these writers challenged the public by their lifestyle as well as their art. Yet the originality that ensued in the art of that time cannot be denied, nor can the deep cry for cultural change be disregarded. Even today the critics differ when it comes to defining Decadent art and the lifestyle of Decadent artists. Questions such as whether decadence was a style or only an attitude arise. Did the Decadents follow a set of rules in their writings, or did they have a point of view to put forth? Finally, were they moral, immoral, or amoral? The fact that the answer is one or all to each individual artist makes Decadent literature rich with research possibilities.

As already noted O'Sullivan was aware that Romanticism revived romance. Harold Bloom argues that "an internalization is made for more than therapeutic purposes, because it is made in the name of a humanizing hope that approaches apocalyptic intensity."[21] Furthermore, Geoffrey Hartman argues that "the desire to gain truth, finality, or revelation generates a thousand such enchantments. Mind has its blissful islands as well as its mountains, its deeps, and its treacherous crossroads. Depicting these trials by horror and by enchantment Romanticism is genuinely a rebirth of Romance."[22] O'Sullivan borrows and varies the Romantic quest by going beyond internalization and turning it into a mystical experience which ultimately, entails the therapy of the soul as it takes its journey through Hell and Purgatory. As he moves from poem to poem and depicts the progress of the persona's soul, he succeeds in showing a simultaneous upward motion to Heaven where the soul is seen fully purified, and where it succeeds in shedding frustrations and pains.

Mysticism and Romanticism seem to be somewhat connected. The former attempts to perceive the unknown, explain the inexplicable relations amongst phenomena, and seek to penetrate all marvels. The latter, by rejecting dry reason and trusting in the imagination as a means of perceiving transcendent reality, acquired a mystical aspect. One can argue without hesitation that O'Sullivan's work is Romantic in form and mystical in content. Hence, it can be argued that his work is a blend of both and that his poetry, though written during the Victorian period, can easily be labeled Romantic. In the following diagram the concepts of Heaven, Purgatory, and Hell are associated with certain psychological as well as mythic and religious ideas. The diagram represents the progress of the persona as he moves from the abyss to heaven where ultimately he achieves the Divine union.

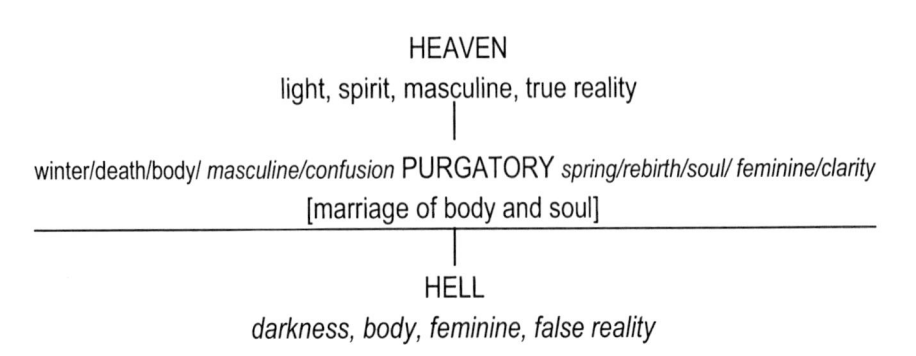

HEAVEN
light, spirit, masculine, true reality
|

winter/death/body/ *masculine/confusion* PURGATORY *spring/rebirth/soul/ feminine/clarity*
[marriage of body and soul]
―――――――――――――――――――――――――――――
|

HELL
darkness, body, feminine, false reality

The diagram also distinguishes between the pairs of body/soul and body/spirit among other pairs of opposites. What should be stressed is first the continuous motion of man's soul. Continuously the soul moves from a lower state to an upward one as it abandons the body and gives in to the spirit through which God hands His grace. At the same time, it also moves from winter to spring, as it is reborn from the death of sin.

Eliade has noted that "every human being tends, even consciously, toward the center, and toward his own center where he can find integral reality-sacredness. This desire that is so deeply rooted in man is the desire to find himself at the very heart of the real at the center of the world."[23] Man's success depends on a constant struggle to rise from darkness into the light of truth. At the same time the danger of falling from light into darkness is ever present. Man has to struggle to discover the true self given to him by God and restored to him by Christ after the fall. Jesus bid Lazarus to return to life and he obeyed and stumbled out from his tomb into the light of day. This very concrete and symbolic episode explains how man is supposed to respond and act at the voice of Christ. In his life man is to stumble from the tomb of lethargy, blindness, doubt, and duplicity into the light at the call of God. Man's soul is to throw off all the bands, which wrap it and impede it from seeing the light of truth as the shroud was shed from Lazarus' body when he returned from the darkness of the grave to the light of day. Similarly, the Romantic hero took a journey of transcendence by rejecting the city which he thought was imperfect and inadequate to find a spiritual life. The Decadents accepted the city and by implication all its temptations as a means of fulfilling his pervert whims and, as a means of transcending into a different reality. As for O'Sullivan the most important preoccupation was taking the mystical journey that would lead to Heaven and God's embrace. Withdrawal was from the outer to the inner world and not from the city to the country. After all, he was concerned with the spirituality of this withdrawal and not with the physical quality of the act.

The struggle between a life wish and a death wish, between the hero's mortal nature and his immortal longings are solid antithesis that underline the quest. O'Sullivan's persona has to go beyond the antithesis of life and death, mortality and immortality. His indecisiveness eventually leads him to make the right decision and thus he takes the path that leads him to Heaven's court and eternal bliss. The persona in O'Sullivan's poetry must abandon all that the physical world has to offer him. He enters of necessity the pit, the cavern, the sea, the wilderness, the nether world, or the tomb. His experience is supposed to liberate him from his fears and from whatever physical demands he has. He must learn to relinquish everything that keeps him bound to the earth.

During his quest the persona is shown spending one ritualistic year which is symbolic of his incarnation. It translates into one complete cycle from spring to winter and from birth to death. When the persona is reborn and returns to earth he bears the tokens of wisdom and power for he can explain the forces of evil and guide whoever is willing to redemption. Symbolically, one year elapses between the first and second volume. In ***The Houses of Sin*** O'Sullivan shows the return of the wise quester who implores the sinner to listen to him and quit his harmful ways. In the first poem *Houses of Sin* he is depicted standing in the corner worried and afraid of the dangers the sinner's soul is about to encounter. The persona's wisdom is about the powers of the soul that help it ascend from the lowest to the highest, go from the exterior to the interior, and pass from the temporal to the eternal. These powers are implanted by nature in man and are, according to Saint Bonaventure: the senses, imagination, reason, understanding, intelligence, and the summit of the mind or the spark of conscience. These powers are usually defiled by sin, but can be purified by grace. So that the man who wants to unite with the Divine must "avoid sin, which deforms [his] nature, exercise his natural powers mentioned above; by praying to receive restoration of grace; [assume] a good life, to receive purifying justice; meditate, to receive illuminating knowledge; and contemplate, to receive perfecting wisdom."[24]

O'Sullivan was of the opinion that religion is the intellectual relation between the finite spirit of man and the infinite spirit of God. Man is related to God in finitude as long as he lives on this earth, and in infinity, through the knowledge he acquires of Him. Hence religion means fearing God and doing His will, it also entails knowing Him through feeling. Finally, man achieves a fundamental reconciliation and a marriage between his soul and God.

From a psychological vantage point, then, there is a great deal of value in those instances where man cannot discriminate between good and evil, or between what is healthy and what is neurotic. Christ clearly recognized this, and on a number of occasions emphasized the importance of accepting evil as part of experience. A good illustration is in the parable of the good and bad seed: "the kingdom of heaven may be compared to a man who sowed good seed in his field ... then gather(ed) the wheat into my barn" (*Matthew* 13. 12-30). This parable interprets the field as the heart of man where evil and good coexist and where, presumably, good will overcome evil. It is an illustration of the medieval psychomachia where the good and evil forces are described locked in continuous conflict, and only when man admits the purifying effect of the Divine spirit could good be enforced and peace prevail.

The Christian myth speaks of how God, Man, and nature were all united until man fell from God and broke the harmony that bound him to nature, but man can be reintegrated if he so wishes. The spiral that leads man down to the center of insight by falling into the sea, symbolizing a return to the mother, can also lead him upward to Heaven. Consequently, it is a mistake to ignore the regenerative powers that lie in the sea, the grave, or, psychologically speaking the unconscious.

The good Christian is a man who believes in Christ and is reborn in Him, for through love he acquires a new life, a Divine life. "You too must consider yourselves to be dead to sin but alive for God in Christ Jesus" (*Romans* 6.11). Man has to become a true child of the Father and he must behave as such. He has the power to do so and henceforth hope since the Son wants him to hope, love as the Son loves, and see as the Son sees. Jesus, it is said, will not take our life if we do not let Him have it. And, once man repents, he should be in continual dialogue with Christ. He must ask Him to rectify and purify his life; he must offer his life to Him so that He may permeate it. Many people regard the soul as being a very beautiful thing, glorious in its various natural qualities, and far grander than any material object. Mortal sin can defile the soul and make it hideous. As long as sin does not taint the soul, it remains resplendent in the glory of God's grace.

Throughout O'Sullivan's poetry there is an everlasting struggle experienced by the persona, between his wish to attain heavenly happiness and the powerful force pulling him downward to a world of sorrow and sensuality. The psychological conflict equates the religious antagonism between Heaven and Hell. It took the persona a while to realize that Heaven could not be achieved before going through the deepest levels of Hell, where his soul would acquire all the purification it needs. Only by diving into the abyss can the soul find freedom. Hence the persona becomes convinced that the downward motion is a way of transcending, and that death is the only means of leading man beyond the grave. Any inklings of doubt he may have had vanished.

In the two volumes O'Sullivan presents and completes the drama of the human soul. In the first volume the soul takes its own journey to purify itself and ends up in the court of Heaven. In the second, the soul returns to guide another soul through the path of righteousness to Heaven. Showing love for another sinner and readiness in saving his soul is a prerequisite for every reborn soul that has found the way to salvation and the path that leads to the union with the Divine. Evidently, the rejuvenated soul has become a "knight" of God and as His messenger he returns to win a soul for the kingdom of Heaven. It is noteworthy that each volume is complete in itself even though the poet uses the metaphor of the soul's mystical journey to link them. The dark night with which **The Houses of Sin** begins shows that the soul has returned to the abyss, the same abyss he succeeded in leaving behind in **Poems**. Furthermore, the place he visits is no other but the desperate and sinful world, a faithful depiction of the society of the nineties, where he meets a sinner whom he tries to save. The reader finds out that the journey of the sinner, along with the persona of the previous volume, leads to the Divine union. The sinner is not told to take a detour or to avoid temptation or sin, nor is he taught ways of resisting temptation. It is as if O'Sullivan has realized that salvation could be achieved only through sin and temptation. Only sin could strengthen man's will, and only tribulations on the bumpy way could strengthen his resolve and lead to redemption. The first volume shows the soul progressing forward and upward to Heaven, while the second volume traces the soul's return to earth. As such the downward motion occurs because the knight of God has only one purpose and that is to save a lost and miserable sinner. Once the soul succeeds in dissolving all the bonds that hampered its motion forward, then it becomes very easy to travel upward. The soul is not afraid of becoming a prisoner anymore. In fact, it seems that the soul gains courage from God and is willing to come to earth repeatedly in order to help save a lost soul that prays and calls for help. The redeemed soul follows Christ's example in coming to earth to save mankind. Having reached the court of Heaven and having lived in the radiance of God's light encourages the newly dubbed knight to prove himself by taking the trip back to earth. His only purpose is to succeed and return victorious with a trophy, in this case, a saved soul. This is the final test the knight has to go through before the union of his soul with the Divine takes place. By looking at the two volumes together one notices a forward and upward motion in **Poems** and a backward and downward motion in **The Houses of Sin**. But at the end of **The Houses of Sin** the motion is reversed to upward since the persona's soul finally unites with the Divine. Saint Teresa describes the union in the following lines:

> This King of Heaven, your Bridegroom He,
> Will give you many jewels rare:
> Wondrous the joys He will prepare
> To comfort you eternally.
> And greatest of His gifts will be
> -Since He can give in royal way-
> A spirit of humility:
> And He's your willing Spouse today.[25]

    The soul of man is in complete defeat and everlasting loss as long as it exists in Hell. There the soul is cut off from any communication with the Saints and is far away from the Atonement of Christ and His charity. Therefore, it is essential that the soul enter Purgatory so as to start communicating with the Saints and receive the grace of God. Once in Purgatory the soul has secured its salvation. Needless to say, that this state is not permanent. And even though it provides a sense of security, still it is not devoid of the most intense pain of being deprived of the sight of God. In Heaven the soul is in bliss because there are no more doubts tearing at it, and no more anguish for being separated from God again. As the purification of the soul goes on, it opens more and more to the influx of God's love, for the sins that defiled it were the only hindrance to the complete union with Him. Gradually, the soul's happiness increases as time goes by, but the agony of being hindered from God and considered unfit for His total and complete love is not, by any means, lessened.

Moreover, O'Sullivan goes one step further by the end of the second volume. The reader does not only witness the persona's soul in Heaven's court but the actual union of the soul with the Divine. The ultimate goal that had encouraged the soul through its hardships is obtained. In *God's Hour* O'Sullivan describes the ascendance of the soul to Heaven as God decides to pull him "up to His white throne" because He has decided to make him a part of Himself. "My will is / That you be Mine own." Throughout the two volumes the soul is led through the kingdom of death, always with the belief that resurrection and immortality are close at hand.

In conclusion, O'Sullivan's poetry is metaphysical because it delineates the mystic path of the pilgrim/persona, the dark nights of the soul, and the final harmony that prevails after the union of the soul with the Divine. This mystical experience forms the subject matter of the two volumes, and is conveyed by a central image depicting God as a Divine Lover that woos the human soul/beloved. The courtship and marriage of the Lover and the Beloved is described both in spiritual as well as erotic terms. O'Sullivan ends this highly personal drama with the desired marriage between the feminine soul, and masculine God. To O'Sullivan, the Holy Marriage of the Bride and the Bridegroom proved the most important cause in man's life. By fusing Catholic views, medieval conventions, and romantic forms, O'Sullivan succeeded in conveying his ideas effectively.

Notes

Chapter IV

[1] Max Nordeau, *Degeneration* (New York: D. Appleton & Co., 1895) 5.

[2] Nordeau 3.

[3] Holbrock Jackson, *The Eighteen Nineties: A Review of Art and Idea at the Close of the Nineteenth Century* (New York: Alfred A. Knopf, 1992) 71.

[4] Nordeau, *Degeneration* 19.

[5] Jackson, *The Eighteen Nineties* 76.

[6] Mircea Eliade, *Images and Symbols: Studies in Religious Symbolism* (New York: Sheed & Ward, 1969) 55.

[7] Ann Belford Ulanov, *The Feminine in Jungian Psychology and in Christian Theology* (Evanston: Northwestern University Press, 1971) 96.

[8] John of the Cross, *The Dark Night of the Soul*, trans. Kurt F. Reinhardt (New York: Frederick Ungar, 1957) 10-12.

[9] M.H. Abrams, *Natural Supernaturalism: Tradition and Revelation in Romantic Literature* (New York: W.W. Norton, 1971) 194.

[10] Heinrich Zimmer and Joseph Campbell eds., *The King and the Corpse: Tales of the Soul's Conquest of Evil* (New Jersey: Princeton University Press, 1937) 44.

[11] Horace E. Scudder ed., *The Complete Poetical Works of Browning* (Massachussettes: Houghton Mifflin Co., 1895) 315.

[12] Joseph C. Pearce, *The Crack in the Cosmic Egg: Challenging Constructs of Mind and Reality* (New York: Simon & Schuster, 1971) 3-4.

[13] James Finley, *Merton's Palace of Nowhere: A Search for God through Awareness of the True Self* (Illinois: Ave Maria Press, 1978) 136.

[14] Thomas à Kempis, *Of the Imitation of Christ: Four Books* (Oxford: Oxford University Press, 1940) 19.

[15] A Kempis 20.

[16] Zimmer, *The King and the Corpse* 35.

[17] Joan Ferrente, *Woman's Image in Medieval Literature: From the Twelfth Century to Dante* (New York: Columbia University Press, 1975) 152.

[18] Harold Bloom, ed., *Romanticism and Consciousness: Essays in Criticism* (New York: W.W. Norton, 1970) 5.

[19] Bloom 6.

[20] Wallace Fowlie, *Love in Literature: Studies in Symbolic Expression* (Indiana: Indiana University Press, 1965) 26-27.

[21] Bloom, *Romanticism and Consciousness* 82.

[22] Hartman, *Romanticism and Consciousness* 54.

[23] Eliade, *Images and Symbols* 82.

[24] Saint Bonaventure, *The Soul's Journey into God*, trans. Ewert Cousins (New York: Paulist Press, 1978) 63.

[25] Saint Teresa, *The Complete Works of Saint Teresa of Jesus*, trans. E. Allisaon Peers (London: Sheed & Ward, 1957) 308.

WORKS CITED

Abrams, M.H. *Natural Supernaturalism: Tradition and Revelation in Romantic Literature*. New York: W.W. Norton, 1971

Baumgart, Winfred. *Imperialism: The Idea and Reality of British and French Colonial Expansion 1880-1914*. Oxford: Oxford University Press, 1982.

Beardsley, Monroe C. *Aesthetics: Problems in the Philosophy of Criticism*. New York: Hackett Publishing Co., 1981.

Berdyaev, Nikolai. *Slavery and Freedom*. New York: Charles Scribner, 1964.

Bloom, Harold. Ed. *Romanticism and Consciousness: Essays in Criticism*. New York: W.W. Norton, 1970.

Carlyle, Thomas. *Sartor Resurtus*. New York: Holt, Rinehart, & Winston, 1970.

Eliade, Mircea. *Images and Symbols: Studies in Religious Symbolism*. New York: Sheed & Ward, 1969.

Ferrente, Joan M. *Woman as Image in Medieval Literature: From the Twelfth Century to Dante*. New York: Columbia University Press, 1975.

Finley, James. *Merton's Palace of Nowhere: A Search for God through Awareness of the True Self*. Notre Dame: Ave Maria Press, 1978.

Fogle, French. *The Complete Poetry of Henry Vaughan*. New York: Anchor Books, 1964.

Fowlie, Wallace. *Love in Literature: Studies in Symbolic Expression*. Indiana: Indiana University Press, 1965.

Gerber, H. C. *Edwardians and Late Victorians*. New

York: Anchor Books, 1986.

Grierson, H. J. C. Ed. *The Poems of John Donne*. Oxford: Oxford University Press, 1966.

Happold, F.C. *Mysticism: A Study and an Anthology*. London: Penguin, 1973.

Hauser, Arnold. *The Social History of Art*. Vol. IV. New York: Vintage, 1978.

Honinghausen, Lothar. *The Symbolist Tradition in English Literature*. Cambridge: Cambridge University Press, 1988.

Houghton, Walter S. *The Victorian Frame of Mind 1830-1890*. Massachussettes: Houghton Mifflin Co., 1968.

Hughes, Merritt.Y. Ed. *John Milton: Complete Poems and Prose*. Indiana: The Odessey Press, 1957.

Jackson, Holbrock. *The Eighteen Nineties: A Review of Art and Ideas at the Close of the Nineteenth Century*. New York: Alfred A. Knopf, 1922.

John of the Cross. *The Dark Night of the Soul*. Trans. Kurt F. Reinhardt. New York: Frederick Ungar Publishing Co., 1957.

Jung, Carl. *The Archetypes of the Collective Unconscious*. New Jersey: Princeton University Press, 1968.

Kamath, M. V. *Philosophy of Death and Dying*. Pennsylvania: Honnesdale Hamalayan International Institute, 1978.

Kelley, Thomas. Ed. *The Fellowship of the Saints: An Anthology of Christian Devotional Literature*. New York: Abingdon Press, 1948.

Lauter, Estelle and Carol Schreier. Eds. *Feminist Archetypal Theory: Interdisciplinary Revisions of*

Jungian Thought. Knoxville: University of Tennessee, 1985.

Lewis, C. S. ***Allegory of Love.*** New York: Oxford University Press, 1958.

Mitchell, Sally. ***Victorian Britain: An Encyclopedia***. New York: Garland Publishing Co., 1988.

Mix, Kathrine Lyon. ***A Study in Yellow***. Kansas: Kansas University Press, 1960.

Miyoshi, Masao. ***The Divided Self: A Perspective of the Literature of the Victorians.*** New York: New York University Press, 1969.

Nordeau, Max. ***Degeneration***. New York: D. Appleton & Co., 1895.

O'Sullivan, Vincent. ***Poems.*** London: Elkin Mathews, 1896.

----------------------. ***The Houses of Sin***. London: Smithers, 1897.

----------------------. ***Aspects of Wilde.*** London: Constable & Co., 1936.

Pater, Walter. ***The Renaissance: Studies in Art and Poetry***. New York: Johnson Co., 1967.

----------------. ***Appreciations.*** London: Macmillan & Co., 1871.

Pearce, Joseph C. ***The Crack in the Cosmic Egg: Challenging Constructs of Mind and Reality.*** New York: Simon & Schuster, 1971.

Pelikan, Jaroslav. Ed. ***Twentieth Century Theology in the Making.*** New York: Fontana, 1971.

Poe, Edgar Allan. ***The Complete Works.*** New York: Thomas Y. Crowell, 1902.

Quoist, Michel. ***Christ is Alive.*** Dublin: Gill and Macmillan,

1971.

Ricks, Christopher. Ed. *The Poems of Alfred Tennyson.* Berkeley: University of California Press, 1987.

Rudrun, Alan. Ed. *The Works of Thomas Vaughan.* Oxford: Clarendon Press, 1984.

Ruskin, John. *Selections from the Writings of John Ruskin.* London: George Allen, 1893.

Saint Bonaventure. *The Soul's Journey into God.* Trans. Evert Cousins. New York: Paulist Press, 1978.

Saint Teresa. *The Complete Works of Saint Teresa of Jesus.* Trans. E. Allison Peers. London: Sheed & Ward, 1957.

Scudder, Horace. Ed. *The Complete Poetical Works of Robert Browning.* Massachussetts: Houghton Mifflin Co., 1895.

Selincourt, Ernest De. Ed. *The Poetical Works of William Wordsworth.* Oxford: Oxford University Press, 1988.

Simpson, Evelyn M. and George C. Potter. Eds. *The Sermons of John Donne.* Vol. VIII. Berkeley: Berkeley University Press, 1954.

Stern, Martin E. and Bert Marino. *Psychotheology: The Discovery of Sacredness in Humanity.* New York: Paulist Press, 1970.

Stott, R.W. *Basic Christianity.* London: Inter-Varsity, 1973.

Summer, Richard and George Roppen. *Strangers and Pilgrims: An Essay on the Metaphor of Journey.* Norway: Norwegian University Press, 1964.

Tagore, Rabindranath. *The Religion of Man.* London: Unwin, 1970.

Thornton, R.K.R. Ed. *Poetry of the Nineties.* London:

Penguin, 1970.

Tindall, W. York. *Forces in Modern British Literature: 1885-1946*. New York: Alfred A. Knopf, 1970.

Tournier, Paul. *The Person Reborn.* London: SCM Heinemann, 1966.

Ulanov, Ann B. *The Feminine in Jungian Psychology and in Christian Theology.* Evanston: Northwestern University Press, 1971.

Walker, Hugh. *The Literature of the Victorian Era.* Cambridge: Cambridge University Press, 1921.

Watts, Alan. *Behold the Spirit.* New York: Vintage Books, 1971.

Waugh, Arthur. Ed. *Samuel Johnson: Lives of the English Poets*. Vol. I Oxford: Oxford University Press, 1952.

Williams George W. Ed. *The Complete Poetry of Richard Crashaw.* New York: Doubleday & Co., 1970.

Winter, David. *Hereafter: What Happens after Death.* Illinois: Harold Shaw Publishers, 1977.

Zimmer, Heinrich and Joseph Campbell. Eds. *The King and the Corpse: Tales of the Soul's Conquest of Evil.* New Jersey: Princeton University Press, 1937.

ALPHABETICAL INDEX

A

A Book of Bargains, 64 (n.)

Abrams, M.H., 201 (n.)

Aesthetics: Problems in the Philosophy of Criticism, 17, 64 (n.)

A Kempis, T., 93, 96, 100, 113, 127 (n.) 136, 137, 176 (n.), 190, 202 (n.)

Allegory of Love, 35, 175 (n.)

Archetypes of the Collective Unconscious, 126 (n.)

Aspects of Wilde, 45, 64, 67 (n.)

Ascent of Mount Carmel, The, 112, 126 (n.)

A Study of English Romanticism, 56

B

Ballad of London, 15

Basic Christianity, 126 (n.), 176 (n.)

Baumgart, W., 64

Beardsley, A., 31

Beardsley, M., 17, 64

Beaudelaire, C., 32, 33

Behold the Spirit, 64, 177 (n.)

Berdayaev, N., 176 (n.), !77 (n.)

Bergson, H., 12, 13

Blake, W., 33

Bloom, H., 58, 191, 193, 202 (n.)

Browning, R., 53, 186

C

Campbell, J., 201 (n.)

Carlyle, T., 16, 64 (n.)

Christ is Alive, 126 (n.), !27 (n.), 176 (n.)

Coleridge, S. T., 95

Collar, The, 106, 158, 169

Communist Manifesto, The, 9

Complete Works of Richard Crashaw, 127 (n.)

Complete Poetry of Henry Vaughan, 127 (n.)

Complete Works of Saint Teresa of Jesus, 202 (n.)

Complete Poetical Works of Robert Browning, 201 (n.)

Crack in the Cosmic Egg: Challenging Constructs of Mind and Reality, The, 201

(n.)

Crashaw, R., 58, 74, 108

D

Dante, A., 35, 191

Dark Night of the Soul, The, 173, 177 (n.), 182, 201 (n.)

Darwin, C., 10, 11

Das Capital, 9

Davidson, J., 15, 41, 42

Degeneration, 10, 201 (n.)

De Selincourt, E., 127 (n.)

Divided Self: A Perspective of the Literature of the Victorians, The, 44

Donne, J., 50, 58, 74, 84, 167

Douglas, A., 15

Dowson, E., 40

Dramatis Personae, 66 (n.)

E

Eckhart, M., 45

Edwardians And Late Victorians, 66 (n.)

Eighteen Nineties, 64 (n.), 65 (n.), 67 (n.), 201 (n.)

Eliade, M., 157, 176 (n.), 181, 194, 201 (n.), 202 (n.)

Epilogue: Credo, 42

Everyman, 132

F

Fellowship of Saints, 128 (n.)

Feminist Archetypal Theory: Interdisciplinary Revisions of Jungian Thought, 64 (n.)

Feminine in Jungian Psychology and in Christian Thought, The, 201 (n.)

Ferrente, J., 67, 68 (n.), 126 (n.), 191, 202 (n.)

Finley, J., 126 (n.), 128 (n.), 149, 176 (n.), 189, 202 (n.)

Fogle, F., 127 (n.)

Forces in Modern British Literature: 1885-1946 65 (n.)

Fowlie, W., 192, 202 (n.)

Freud, S., 13, 14

Frye, N., 54, 56, 68 (n.)

G

Gerber, H., 26, 66

Gissing, G., 15, 26

Good Friday Riding Westward, 167

Grierson, H.J.C., 68 (n.), 177

(n.)

Good Girl, The, 64 (n.)

H

Happold, F.C., 67, 68 (n.), 127 (n.)

Hardy, T., 26

Hartman, G., 193, 202 (n.)

Hauser, A., 66

Heiddeger, M., 30

Hereafter, 164, 177 (n.)

Herbert, G., 58, 74, 105, 106, 158, 169

Hildegarde of Bingen, 123

Honinghausen, L., 19, 64

Houghton, W.S., 67 (n.)

Houses of Sin, 55, 64 (n.), 131, 132, 133, 134, 174, 176 (n.), 184, 185, 192, 196, 198, 199

Houses of Sin: *Remnants* 132, 171; *Houses of Sin* 134; *Malaria* 138; *The House of the Ghosts* 139; *The Verge* 140; *Drug* 141; *Three Moments* 142; *Love in Tears* 144; *The Dancer at the Opera* 145; *Woman of the Mist* 146, 147; *Shadows* 147; *The Children of Wrath* 147; *Fear at Night* 149; *Our Lady of the Fields* 150; *Francis Borgia at Grenada* 151; *Calvary Hill* 152, 158; *Hymn to May* 155; *At the Gate of the Year* 156; *The Full Moon* 156; *A Silken Ladder* 157, 158, 160; *The Lonely Woman* 162; *A Slave of the Street* 163; *To an Enemy: when Dying* 164; *A Prayer* 165, 169; *The Rivals* 58, 166; *The Voices of the Winds* 167; *God's Hour* 169, 200; *For the End* 170

Housman, A.E., 26

Hughes, M.Y., 69 (n.), 176 (n.)

Hughes, S.H., 64 (n.)

Hutchinson, F.E., 127 (n.)

I

Images and Symbols: Studies in Religious Symbolism, 99, 176 (n.), 201 (n.), 202 (n.)

Imperialism: The Idea and Reality of British and French Colonial Expansion 1880-1914, 64 (n.)

Impressions Du Nuit, 15

Intimations to Immortality: An Ode, 43

J

Jackson, H., 10, 21, 64 (n.), 67 (n.), 201 (n.)

John Milton: Complete Poems and Prose, 176 (n.)

Johnson, L., 40

Jung, C., 14, 23, 47, 68 (n.), 126 (n.)

K

Kamath, M.V., 114, 126 (n.), 127 (n.)

Kelley, T., 67 (n.), 68 (n.)

L

Lady of Shalott, The, 30

Last Music, The, 15

Lauter, E,. 64

Le Gallienne, R., 15

Lewis, C. S., 35, 66

London, 15

Literature of the Victorian Era, The, 38

Love in Literature: Studies in Symbolic Expression, 202 (n.)

M

Man's Search for Himself, 68 (n.)

Marino, B., 113, 127 (n.)

May, R., 52, 68 (n.)

Merton's Palace of Nowhere: A Search for God through Awareness of the True Self, 126 (n.), 128 (n.), 176 (n.), 202 (n.)

Milton, J., 61, 137

Mitchell, S., 64 (n.)

Mix, K.L., 66 (n.)

Miyoshi, M., 44, 67 (n.)

Morris, W., 9

Mysticism: A Study and an Anthology, 127 (n.)

N

Natural Supernaturalism: Tradition and Revelation in Romantic Literature, 201 (n.)

Nietzsche, F., 11,12,13

Nihilism, 41

Nordeau, M., 10,17,64 (n.), 179, 180, 201 (n.)

O

Of the imitation of Christ: Four Books, 127 (n.), 176 (n.),

177 (n.), 202 (n.)

On Style, 25

"O Mors! Quam Amora Est Memoria Tua Homini Pacem Habenti in Substantis Suis," 67(n.)

On the Origin of Species, 10

P

Paradise Lost, 61, 137

Pater, W., 15, 22, 23, 25, 42, 43, 53, 65 (n.), 67 (n.) 132

Pearce, J., 188, 201 (n.)

Pelikan, J., 69 (n.)

Person Reborn, The, 68 (n.)

Piligrim's Progress, 132

Plato, 43

Poe, E. A., 27, 33, 66 (n.)

Poems, 55, 64 (n.), 73, 123, 126 (n.), 131, 132, 134, 135, 171, 181, 185, 188, 192, 198, 199

Poems; *To his Soul 73; According to Mercy 76; Knight of Dreams 77; Norman Cradle Song 80; Lament 81; By the Sea-Well 84, 90, 94; The Peace of God 85; A Cold Night 86; Rose Witchery 87; Pirate Wife's Song 88; The Lady 89; White Dreaming 90; Children's Hymn on the Coast of Brittany 90; Ariadne 91; Papillions du Pavé 35, 91; Unto the Throne 92; Two Voices 94; Dirge 94; Brain Fever 95; In Window-lights 95; Sea Sounds 97; Caitiff's Rhyme 97; Fairy's Music 97; Old Mother's Lull-to-Sleep 99 ; A Triumph 101, 192; Hermit's Harrow 103; Night Voyaging 103; The Cathedral 104; In the Road 105; Wheat and Clover 106, 191; Lake Glamour 108; In the Hymn to St. Dominick 108; Woman's Song 109; Garden Fantasy 109; On a Day 111; Sancta Dei Genetrix 111; Spring 112, 114; Hymn of the Norman Sailors 113; The Statue of St. Vincent de Paul in Amiens Cathedral 114; Breton Lullaby 115; Hymn to our Lady of Peace 116; The Angelus 117; Widow's Croon 118; The End of Years 119; Nights of Dreaming 119, The Veil of Light 120; Momento Homo Quia Pulvis Es 122; Envoi 123*

Poetry of the Nineties, 67 (n.)

Potter, G.C., 127 (n.)

Price, The, 42

Psychotheology: The discovery of Sacredness in Humanity, 127 (n.)

Q

Quoist, M., 126 (n.), 159, 176 (n.)

R

Religion of Man, The, 30

Regeneration, 85, 158

Renaissance, 25

Revelations, 172, 184,

Ricks, C., 66 (n.)

Rimbaud, A., 32, 33

Romanticism and Consciousness: Essays in Criticism, 202 (n.)

Roppen, G., 68 (n.)

Rosetti, G., 27

Rudrun, A., 177

Ruskin, J., 16, 27, 53, 66 (n.)

Ruysbrock, 45

S

Saint Augustine, 64 (n.)

Saint Augustine, 37, 39, 64, 170, 189

Saint Bonaventure, 80, 108, 126 (n.), 127 (n.), 196, 202 (n.)

Saint John of the Cross, 71, 72, 112, 126 (n.), 158, 159, 173, 177 (n.), 182, 190, 201 (n.)

Samuel Johnson: Lives of the English Poets, 69 (n.)

Sartor Resartus, 64 (n.)

Schreiner, C., 64

Scudder, H., 201 (n.)

Selections from the Writings of John Ruskin, 66 (n.)

Shaw, G. B., 16, 26

Sermons of John Donne, 127 (n.), 202 (n.)

Simpson, E., 127

Slavery and Freedom, 176 (n.), 177 (n.)

Social History of Art, The, 66 (n.)

Soul Afire, The, 123

Soul's Journey into God, The, 126 (n.)

Spenser, E., 54

Spenser, H., 10

Stern, M.E., 113, 127 (n.)

Stevenson, R.L., 15

Stott, R.W., 126 (n.), 176 (n.)

Strangers and Pilgrims: An Essay on the Metaphor of Journey, 68 (n.)

Studies in Art and Prose, 66 (n.)

Summer, R., 68 (n.)

Swinburne, A., 15

Symbolist Tradition of English Literature, 65 (n.)

Symons, A., 15, 31, 32, 42, 66 (n.), 179

T

Tagore, R., 30, 66 (n.)

Tennyson, A., 30

Teresa of Avila, 202 (n.)

Temple, The, 105

Tindall, W.Y., 64

Thompson, F., 15

Thornton, R.K.R., 67 (n.)

Tournier, P., 68 (n.), 149, 176 (n.)

Transition, 40

Twentieth Century Theology in the Making, 69 (n.)

U

Ulanov, A.B., 201 (n.)

V

Vaughan, H., 74, 85, 105, 158

Vaughan, T., 174

Verlaine, P., 8, 32

Victorian Britain: An Encyclopedia, 65 (n.)

W

Walker, H., 38, 175 (n.)

Watts, A., 168, 177 (n.)

Waugh, A., 69 (n.)

Whistler, J.M., 16

Wilde, O., 15, 16, 27, 42, 45, 53, 132

Williams, G.W., 127 (n.)

Winter, D., 164, 177 (n.)

Woman Archetype in Medieval Literature: From the Twelfth Century to Dante, 126 (n.), 202 (n.)

Wordsworth, W., 99

Works of George Herbert, 127 (n.)

Works of Thomas Vaughan, 177 (n.)

Y

Yellow Book, The, 16

Z

Zimmer, H., 177 (n.), 185, 190, 201 (n.), 202 (n.)